The Book on Selling

Written by Dan Janjigian

Copyright © 2022 by Dan Janjigian All rights reserved.

No portion of this book may be reproduced in any form without written permission from the publisher or author, except as permitted by U.S. copyright law.

Dedication

Writing this book was a lot more difficult than I could have imagined, and it couldn't have been done without the help and support of some amazing people. First off, thanks to my Mom, and professional editor, Florence Janjigian who dug through multiple revisions of The Book on Selling, and helped focus my thoughts in a way that was easier on the reader.

Thanks to my mentor, Jeff Rogers for your counsel in every major business and life decision I've made, including creating and publishing this book. You've been a "north star," in my journey through life, and what you've shared with me and others has been life changing.

Special thanks to Rick Altig, the founder of AO, for his guidance and support. Rick, you're the definition of what it means to be successful in business and especially with family. You really are an inspiration for what's possible.

Eric Hemati, thank you for writing the forward to TBoS, but more than that, thanks for your friendship and your partnership both in and out of business. Your family is an important part of our lives, and I can't wait to see what's next!

Thanks to the rest of my family, my Dad, Aram, who showed me what entrepreneurial spirit really looks like. My brother Michael and his incredible wife Yelena and my two beautiful nieces, Izzy and Audrey who exemplify family. My sister Lori for her 100% support of both her brothers, and being one of my BBF. My kids, Landon, Jenica and Nevi, who I live for, and are growing into amazing young adults, and of course our dogs, Casey and Cat, both of which are always bringing positive vibes into the house.

Last but not least, I want to thank my KM crew, Billy Cunningham, Angela Morrow, Jen Murray, Ara Bezdjian, Mark Suzuki, Mike Herkenrath, Jason Clark, Cal Smith, Adom Moutafian and Nick Seewar, for their continued friendship through all these years. You guys are my old guard, and the newly added guard of Kels Farmer, Jamie, Hourahan, Scott Fuller, Greg Ganske, are all the crew I'd go to war with. Love you guys, and here's to many more years of great memories, and helping serve each other.

DON'T FORGET TO GRAB YOUR FREE BOOK!

https://www.thebookonselling.net/

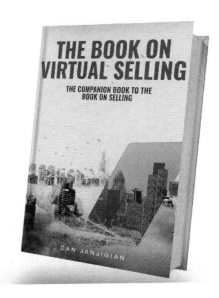

The Book On Virtual Selling:
The companion book to The Book On Selling

Learn how to maximize the shift to online selling without losing the human touch.

Contents

Foreword 5
Preface 9
Chapter 1: Training Camp 15
Chapter 2: The Law of Averages 17
Chapter 3: Actors on a Stage 19
Chapter 4: The Cycle of Sales 21
Chapter 5: Pre-Approach 23
Chapter 6: Approach 33
Chapter 7: The Introduction: AKA Establishing Rapport and the Need...43
Chapter 8: The Buying Atmosphere 55
Chapter 9: The Demonstration 59
Chapter 10: The Price Buildup 67
Chapter 11: The Close 77
Chapter 12: Rebuttals 83
Chapter 13: Collecting Cash 91
Chapter 14: Referrals 95
Chapter 15: Reservicing 107
Chapter 16: Various Methods of Direct Sales 117
Chapter 17: Setting Up Business Enrollments 123
Chapter 18: The Grass Always Looks Greener 127
Chapter 19: Integrity 131
Chapter 20: Let's Go! 135
Chapter 21: Bonus for Managers 137

Foreword

"Who is that guy??" I asked. Across the bar a commotion was unfolding around a tall, unusually fit man in a black skull-cap as he hugged and greeted the rest of my crew. As he reached out and shook my hand firmly, with a big smile he announced, "Hi I'm Danny!"

It would be years later that I would discover I had just met the legendary "Chris R." from "The Room". That handshake was the beginning of a lifelong friendship and a professional collaboration that continues to this day.

We both got our start in sales the same way - our immigrant, Middle-Eastern fathers taught us how to *hustle*. Phrases like "Son, there's no free lunch!", and "What? You think that money grows on a tree??" were commonly heard bouncing their way down our ear canals and into our little minds. Sharing memories with each other, we discovered the most important one for both of us was, ""*Can't*" isn't a word in this house." We both learned at a young age that to get money we would have to come up with something of value that other people would want to pay us for - whether that was mowing the lawn, raking leaves, or selling clocks door-to-door (really!).

When we were in college, we both were recruited to do a summer internship selling educational books door-to-door for straight commission. We both excelled at it - becoming not just top salespeople, but top recruiters and team-leaders as well. By the time we each left college, we had been in thousands of closing situations and stacked up well into six-figures in commissions before most of our peers had even lined up their first interviews.

We met in the insurance business. A good week with that first company we worked with was $10,000 in sales - they called it "Writing an Eagle." You would even get to write up the story of how the week had gone and how you were able to pull together so much business. They would then publish that story and send it out to the entire sales force. In any given week, there would only be a couple of Eagles out of over 2,000 agents.

One of my favorite memories was from a road-trip we took to South Texas. We would do these trips where we'd get a bunch of agents in a hotel for a week where we didn't have much market penetration. The strategy was to fan out into the surrounding small towns to knock on doors and introduce ourselves and our products to the community. I always thought it remarkable that people still would buy things that way, but it was incredibly effective. And if you were any good at it, it was a real blast to meet new people and help them solve problems they didn't even know they had before they met you.

Wednesday evening, Dan was headed back to the hotel around 9pm. He was glowing (that's when you're smiling ear-to-ear on the outside AND the inside) because he had written an Eagle *in just one day*. He was going to be #1 in the room. And once the national numbers came in, he could be #1 in the whole country that day!

When I was told the news, I was (of course) so happy for him. And happier for ME, since I had outsold him that day with over $11,000 ;-)

But as we were getting ready to take a selfie with me holding up one (#1) finger and him holding up two, our friend Jack walked in the restaurant with over $13,000 for the day - the joke was on BOTH of us! Here's the picture we ended up taking that day:

But Dan ended up having the last laugh that week. After all was said and done, he had written over $68,000 in new business and set the all-time company record for weekly sales. He's a great sport ... and he hates to lose. I think that's the thing I've admired most about Dan during the journey we've shared together - he's ALWAYS willing to play the game. He believes he's going to win and he's going to leave it all out on the field to make that win happen, but regardless of the outcome, he always learns something, has a blast, and is ready to play again.

Over the years I've seen Dan be a salesman, a sales trainer, a sales manager, an Olympian, a politician (almost didn't include that in the list, but we all make mistakes), a bartender, a public speaker, husband, a father, a single dad, a motorcycle rider, and an actor. He's owned a web development company, a wedding dress company, a live music venue, a restaurant, a software and app development company, and two insurance agencies. He also has the distinction of being the very best actor in the very *worst* movie ever made in Hollywood.

And through all those years, all those roles, and all of life's ups and downs that go with them, he's been a true and loyal friend and confidant and I'm incredibly grateful I've been privileged to have him in my life.

I've often thought of "sales" as "the art of making things happen." And through the pages that follow, you will learn the techniques and tactics that Dan has used to make so many things happen in his life and in the lives of the people who have worked with him. But more importantly, I hope you soak up a bit of his heart - because that is what has made him so extraordinarily effective.

Enjoy the journey!

Eric Hemati

Preface

In 1977, I closed my first sale at age five. My parents owned a little Armenian restaurant in Sunnyvale, California, and if you've ever heard the term "family restaurant," this was it. The Armenian Gourmet had a small dining area with an even smaller kitchen. An 8-track played music, and my dad kept a canvas bag of coins under the register, which I'd always dig through for bicentennial "drummer boy" quarters for my grandmother. The tables were covered with black-and-white tablecloths with clear plastic over them. From as far back as I can remember, we had to work at the restaurant whenever we didn't have something else of "value" to do.

At that age, I still remember going up to a table and my mom directing me to ask the customers what they wanted for dessert: homemade baklava or cheesecake. She didn't say "Ask them *if* they want dessert." I presented two options and asked them to pick one. They usually went for the baklava, and I had my first lesson in salesmanship.

During elementary and high school, I stuck with sales, going door to door to create a Grit Newspaper subscription base and sold personalized stationery from a membership off the back of a comic book. A little cashbox held my money, and a notebook served as a check register to track what I was taking in and spending.

In June of 1992, having just completed my freshman year at Cal Poly, San Luis Obispo, I was recruited for a summer job on the opposite coast selling educational books to families with kids. The day after finals, we drove in a caravan—44 hours to Nashville, Tennessee—to start our week of training with the Southwestern Company.

There were about 20 of us from school, and Sandee Mathews, our student manager, walked us though what the week would look like. Basically, it was a seven-day pep rally where we learned the cycle of sales, simultaneously becoming committed to each other, our goals, and the idea of doing something that pushed us to our limits for 14 straight weeks. About four thousand college students would be doing the same that year.

After the training week ended with an amazing keynote by Mort Utley, my group drove to South Plainfield, New Jersey, where we were tasked with knocking on doors to find a place to live for the summer.

"Hi, I'm sorry to bother you, but I'm a college student from California out here with some friends to work for the summer and raise money for school. We're not here to party. Frankly, we're gone every day by about 6:30 a.m. and don't get back until late. We're looking for a safe place to lay our heads every night. Would you happen to have a room or two available?"

I still can't believe that every year we found lodging in that way, but that's the sales talk we used to make it happen.

Now, it's the end of my fourth week of sales, and I'm standing in front of Mike Hampton's house. I've spoken to his wife, Sarah, a couple of times during the week, but she's not interested in seeing anything without her husband's presence. It's about 10 p.m. on Saturday night, and I'm sitting on 480 units of sales for the week. To make Presidents Club, I've got to hit 500. It's dark out, and I'm supposed to be meeting with my team. At this ridiculous hour, I'm standing on Mike's porch, knocking.

"Can I help you?!" Mike asks gruffly as he opens the front door.

"Hey, Mike, my name is Dan, and I'm a college student from California...."

He cuts me off, "What do you want?!"

"I'm sorry! Sarah asked me to come back. I guess you haven't heard about me yet...," I start.

"WHAT DO YOU WANT?" he demands, raising his voice.

"Iie yo vendo libre!" I respond with a big smile, flinging my arms out wide. I'd picked up the phrase from one of my other Italian clients, and prayed I was saying it right.

"I am the bookman!" I repeated, smiling but really nervous.

He looked at me, looked at my bookbag, looked at me again, started lightly shaking his head and said,

"Come on in."

Welcome to President's Club.

This isn't a book to "pump you up" with lots of concepts and ideas to get you excited to go to work and stop procrastinating. I'm writing this to share practical ideas to use today in your sales and nuances to be aware of as you master the sales cycle. Understand: All sales are conceptually the same, although the cycle might be longer or shorter depending on what you're selling. A seller of luxury jets or major real estate deals will, in most cases, have a longer sales cycle because of many decision makers and hands in the deal, than someone selling vacuums, insurance, or alarm systems door to door to a family. Keep that in mind as we break down each chapter.

And—if you're new to sales—be comfortable with discomfort. Sales is one of the most lucrative professions out there, but the reason that everyone doesn't do it is because most people are not okay with discomfort. The fear of rejection—and sometimes even the fear of success—can be overwhelming, and there's an odd comfort in just going out, getting a J.O.B., and simply doing what we're told.

I've never liked the idea of an ordinary job because it constitutes a level of babysitting. Whether you're an executive or just starting, someone's eye is always on you. You came in late. You left early. They review your performance and, based on that, fire you or lay you off. Business slows or something happens in the industry, and you're out.

Never does a salaried position have any level of security. Conversely, a company will seldom if ever lay off its top salespeople. If sales stop, the company stops. That's power. If you're at a company that treats its salespeople right, then that power is well compensated. Being a direct salesperson who's on 100% commission is even better because it means that you're the boss. You eat what you kill, and that has built-in benefits. You vacation when you please. You set your own hours. You're more flexible and can do more with your time. Granted, if you don't sell, you have no income, but after reading this book, I hope you understand one key point: If you work, you will sell. PERIOD. You may have *days* of nonproduction, but top salespeople will prove that you'll never have *weeks* of nonproduction. The law of averages will see to that.

How to Read This Book
The Book on Sales comprises several parts. A manager or salesperson can use this book in various ways. First, read it cover to cover. Sense the flow of how the cycle works and learn to transition from one segment to the next. Recognize the nuances that lead to greater closing rates and learn helpful concepts for when you hit a wall and feel defeated.

Review any of these ideas by simply referring to the pertinent chapter where you or one of your salespeople need help. Each chapter stands on its own, so review several times if you sense something missing in a presentation. Study a chapter before bedtime and again during breakfast the next morning. After three weeks, you won't need to "reach" for the information that's being shared. The true test of your skill in any of these areas is your *retention* of the material so that you can effectively respond to what your prospect is saying, and the emotions being expressed. Until you become proficient, you're basically walking through the woods of your sale blindfolded.

A New Kind of Sales
In 2020, the world was hit with a major pandemic that changed the way many of us pursued direct sales. Instead of knocking on doors, we made web conferencing calls, sold via the phone, or found ways to work in person

while "social distancing" from our clients. The way we'd demonstrate fundamentally changed, and we were forced to zig and zag because we didn't know if things would ever go back to the way they were. Even though our platform for selling may have changed, the fundamental rules of sales that this book takes you through have not.

This book is meant to pass on tangible ideas that you can use to learn the art of sales, or even master the art within your specific market. Although the majority of this book will share practices that you can implement into building a sales strategy, or improving your current process, there will be conceptual information as well. Will positive self-talk create a sales talk? No…. Will it help you become a better salesperson? ABSOLUTELY.

Chapter 1

"If one advances confidently in the direction of his dreams, and endeavors to live the life which he has imagined, he will meet with a success unexpected in common hours"

Thoreau

Training Camp

Anyone *can* excel at sales, but not everyone *will*. The adage that you can teach skill but not will is never truer than when it relates to sales. Nothing is more uncomfortable than direct sales, which is why it pays so well. There are countless inside sales jobs, customer service positions, and so on, but those pale in comparison to direct sales. Direct salespeople *create* business where it didn't exist before. An inside sales rep may be great at upselling, but the client called *them* and was already a prospect. Direct salespeople knock on a door, enter a business, or make a phone call to create or fill a need that didn't exist prior to that contact. That's power.

Building a Strong Foundation
With any product or service, you need an intimate understanding of that "thing" to really get excited about it. You can't truly get excited about anything unless you know something about it. If you're selling insurance and you know that your product can protect someone experiencing cancer, *and*

the premiums are refundable if they don't need it, *that's* exciting, but it's just the start. You must believe and learn the responses to common objections that arise. You know that your product or service sounds "too good to be true," so your *trust* in what you're selling becomes a factor. You may simply need to adjust or fine-tune your presentation so that it clearly demonstrates the customer's need for what you're selling.

Allow yourself the time to get out and practice until you become proficient. It's okay to be bad, with the understanding that you'll get better. Because they're rusty, on their first day of training camp, returning football players don't perform at the same level they did the previous season. Back on the field against some good competition, they hone their skills before the season begins.

You're no different. Get out in front of prospects to practice your demonstration. Don't practice in front of a mirror or with your spouse and think that it's as effective as getting in front of a prospect who might actually purchase from you. Many new salespeople want as much time as possible following another agent or learning in the office in a classroom-like setting. This has some value in the very beginning to learn the basics but let me make this crystal clear: *You are wasting time.*

To learn to ride a bike, you could study videos, manuals, and flashcards and memorize step-by-step instructions on getting on and off, the best methods for peddling, and maybe even how to pop a wheelie, *but…* (and you already know what's coming): Nothing holds a candle to your actually getting on a bike and getting familiar with it. You'll never understand the balance required, how to maneuver, or any of the nuances of bike riding unless you get on the damn thing and skin your knees a little. Once you get it, though—it's just like riding a bike!

Get in the field. You'll never be prepared enough. You'll never know the product as well as you'd like to. You'll feel nervous and vulnerable. Accept all of that. Embrace it. Again, be comfortable with your discomfort. The only way to eliminate your fear is with action that you sustain for 21 days to truly create a habit that rids your fear and leads to success.

Chapter 2

"Don't judge each day by the harvest you reap but by the seeds that you plant"

Robert Louis Stevenson

The Law of Averages

This isn't Webster's definition, but here's a metaphor. If you take a bag of cow manure and knock on enough doors, someone will eventually buy it. It might be for compost or just because they're into weird purchases, but *someone* will buy. If you believe that (and you should!), then you understand that the better your product or service, the higher percentage of sales you'll make.

Direct selling is no different. If you sell a product that has a 20% close rate, that means that companywide, one out of every five demonstrations result in a sale. You might not close one out of every five, but if you have average presenting abilities, the more presentations you make, the sooner you'll reach that average. The goal is simple: See as many prospects as you can in the least amount of time.

Marbles on a Pool Table

Working efficiently is the most important aspect of excelling in your sales numbers. Call the top seller in your industry and ask how many prospects they see in a week or a month and compare that to your number. Here's the interesting thing. Let's say they see 20 prospects a week, and you only see five, but you're out there working the same number of hours. You feel as if you're working hard, but you might be mistaking motion for productivity. Ultimately, you will see that same number of prospects—but it takes you a month. Even if you average the same size of sale, the top seller makes in one week what it took you a month to make. You don't need to get better in sales; you need to become more efficient.

When you're in the field, imagine a pool table with no pockets and replacing the felt with a map of your sales territory. Now imagine scattering a bag of marbles over the map. Some areas would have clumps of marbles, others not many, but, in general, marbles would be scattered all over your territory.

Think of those marbles as potential sales. Your job is to move through your territory as efficiently and quickly as possible to get to those marbles. In some areas, you might have many potential buyers; in others, none, but, generally, they'll be scattered about. Now, does finding the marbles guarantee the sale? No, so here's the catch:

You need the right *attitude* once you find a marble (prospect). If your attitude isn't right, then the prospect most likely will not become a client. Efficiency is one thing, but what makes the difference with the prospect? Your attitude when you're in front of them.

Working in sales, you build up calluses just as you would in a construction job. Ever look at the hands of construction workers? They could probably work without gloves because their palms are just thicker and have adapted to constant stresses. Martial artists experience the same phenomenon. If you or I were to block a blow with our forearms, we'd probably get pretty bruised up. True martial artists practice getting hit so often that they seldom bruise because their bodies have become accustomed to taking those blows.

As a sales professional, your *attitude* should build similar calluses, because calluses don't bruise easily. Learn to approach each new prospect with a fresh outlook and renewed passion. They deserve that.

Chapter 3

*"We make a living by what we get, we make
a life by what we give."*

Winston Churchill

Actors on a Stage

Salespeople who regularly perform at the top of their game have two distinct characteristics that are key to mastering their product or service.

Confidence
Confidence begins at the door. The "door" might be a phone in the case of a caller, the admin at a business, or simply the front door of someone's home. In all cases, create an out-of-body experience for yourself and observe your approach demeanor. This self-awareness is difficult when you start with a new product, service, or company, but ask yourself, "Would I let me in?" Would you? If you knocked on your own door, and your family didn't know you, would your wife be comfortable enough with you to let you in? Are you nervous and sweating, or confident and genuine? People like to be around other good people; it's human nature. But if you don't appear confident, it makes people nervous. Again, would *you* let you in?

Conviction

Please, please, *please* only sell something that you love or truly believe in. There are lots of great companies, and I've been lucky enough to work in some amazing organizations, but the one common denominator is having a passion for the products I've sold. People sense your conviction, and if they're on the fence regarding your product, *conviction* will generally produce the swing vote for them.

If you don't know why your client should have your product, even more than *they* do, then you're not convicted enough in what you're selling. You're thinking more about your commission check than you are about the client's needs.

Confidence and conviction make for the best stage performances. Would I rather go to an opening night performance or see a show a few weeks in? I always opt for the latter because in the first few shows, the actors are still perfecting their lines, getting comfortable with the sets, and building chemistry with their fellow actors. After a few weeks, they *know* their lines and are familiar with their surroundings. Now they can really play off the other actors: listen and react; not just think about what to say or do next.

You expect the actors' best performance, even if they've done three shows already that day. You expect emotion and passion. Should *your* presentation be less passionate? When selling, learn the words, perfect the nuances, and deliver your presentation with conviction the fifth time in a day as enthusiastically as the first. Your prospect deserves that.

If you think that acting is a weak metaphor because what you do isn't "pretend"—you're wrong. Selling is transference of feeling. Your prospects are buying *you* as much as they're buying the product. If you sincerely love what you're selling, then deliver that feeling each time that you present. You'll give your prospects the best opportunity to buy.

Chapter 4

"Inches make champions"

Vince Lombardi

The Cycle of Sales

The cycle of sales is a series of landmarks in the process of closing a deal on a product or a service. It's called a cycle because when you're finished, it leads you into the next deal. "Rinse and repeat" so to speak. Visit a prospect, let that lead you to the next prospect, and then the next. Cold calling is not only important, but as you'll see as we break down the cycle, cold calling is *vital* to filling in gaps when you don't have another prospect lined up. True growth in business is in referrals and reservicing your current client base.

Examining the cycle, you will recognize the variety of places that it's used in everyday life. Think about the nontraditional ways that we sell every day:

- A teacher needs to sell the students on the importance of learning the day's algebra lesson.
- A college student wants to sell a woman in his class on having dinner with him.
- A wife needs to sell her husband on a trip that the family should take together.

- A teen needs to sell her parents on why she should be able to go to the mall with her friends.

Sales surrounds us in everything that we do, and the cycle of sales relates to all situations, although our focus may change. The next chapters break down the different parts of the sales cycle, so as you read, select what's most useful to you today. Don't feel that you must "eat the elephant" and figure it all out, but as you go through these sections, focus on pertinent chapters that will help drive you forward. Skip over sections that don't pertain to you.

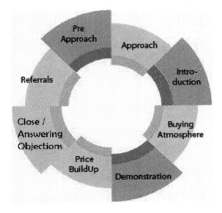

Chapter 5

"A life is not important except in the impact it has on other lives"

Jackie Robinson

Pre-Approach

The first step in the cycle of sales is to pre-approach your prospect; that is, get some reconnaissance on who you're going to talk to. If you're working door to door, find out about the upcoming houses and even the houses that were vacant when you dropped by. Business to business (B2B) is basically the same, and the concept of pre-approach can also be tied to referrals, which we'll break down later.

Pre-approach is key because it moves you from the level of a solicitor to a professional. When you approach a client, you'll always demand more respect if you know something about them. Their name is a good start. If you're selling to a business, know what it does or sells. If you're selling kids' books, do they have kids? If you're selling alarms, are they in a high-crime area? All these bits of information are called pre-approach, and it's the most important component that sets you apart, especially if you're cold calling.

Mapping

When preparing pre-approach, have an organized way of tracking and quickly referencing that information. Map your territory. Decide if you're going to track on a notepad or through one of several apps that are available commercially. Most of the best apps aren't free, but, depending on your product or service, they can simplify your job. Two of my favorites are:

- Sales Navigator—Apple iOS-based service
- Spotio—Internet-based service (needs a connection)

These are great apps, but nothing beats the price and convenience of putting pen to paper. It's quick, easy to reference, and for cold calling, lets you work and figure things out quicker than any app. If you're working phones or virtually, there are unlimited CRM's (Customer Relation Management tools) that you can use. Let's attack the pre-approach from the perspective of door-to-door sales, as the same rules apply across the board.

When you're working door to door, even if you run into a client that isn't interested, your first go-to is to always ask for help. Most people love to help, even if they're not interested in what you're selling. Referring to Chapter 3, exude confidence, or people will feel uncomfortable sharing information with you and may feel like you're stalking their neighborhood rather than offering a product of value. In addition, be effusively thankful as they're sharing information.

Some Rules to Pre-Approach

1) **Start with general questions**: It's easy to start broad and then get specific. If you're selling Medicare programs and are specifically looking for older folks, ask if the people next door are older *before* you ask their names. That's an easy, safe question for anyone to answer.
2) **Develop a rapport with the person who's helping you**. Find something to chat about as you're taking notes, and it's a bonus to laugh with them. Rapport creates comfort, which will get you more information.

3) **Get information on as many houses as you can.** Don't quit at just their next-door neighbors. If you can get information on every house down the street, then do it. The more you get, the less you'll have to fill in later, and the more professional you'll appear.

4) **Don't get too specific.** Recognize your audience. Some people will happily share the name of their neighbors, the ages of the kids, and all sorts of stuff. Others won't want to share

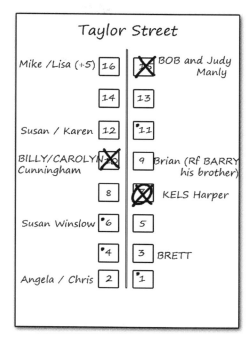

a thing. In all cases, always be appreciative of their time. The goal is to leave everyone better than before you found them. *Never* get into an argument; it won't lead to anything positive for you.

5) **Don't be afraid to waste paper.** Your notes are important, so leave *plenty* of room. I've seen people try to fit multiple streets on a small note pad, and that's crazy. Have plenty of room so you can quickly reference the information you need and make it legible. Write with a normal font size; don't make yourself need to buy reading glasses.

6) **Develop your own shorthand.** If you speak to someone, write their names in all CAPS to distinguish them from another person you simply got the name of. Use +6 or -6 to remind yourself if you need to go back after 6 or before 6. Jot down referrals, relationships you want to remember, or even stories that will help you personalize your approach. Note down items that will help you quickly recognize the house (this is especially important if you're trying to find

appointments at night). Maybe it's a circular driveway, a Tweety Bird mailbox, or a bunch of toys in the front yard. Sometimes references like this are more valuable than house numbers.

7) **Map in the direction that you'll drive your territory.** When selling door to door, the most effective way to work a territory is by working a circuit. People come home at different times of the day, so if you're in your car, you should easily be able to track your maps as you're driving, because you'll be covering the same track at least three or four times. I start my streets at the bottom of the page and work my way up, continuing the map on the next page. As I'm driving, I simply flip the page at the end of the street. The same is true with side streets.

8) **Track your wins**! Make sure to jot down the houses you've already visited (calls), the houses you've demonstrated to, and the houses you've sold to. To truly work an area "tight," you want to continue to go back until you've caught every prospect. The tighter you work, the higher quality the remaining houses become. The reason this is true is because you'll know all the neighbors, you'll have had several sales in the area, and you'll feel more comfortable because you're now a veteran on that street. The way I personally track is by putting a mark on the box that I draw for the house:

   a. An approach is a big dot
   b. A demo is a big X
   c. A sale is a big X with an O around it

Pre-Approaching a New Area

There's no such thing as a bad territory. You'll find great people in what you perceive as bad territory, and horrible people in what you perceive to be great territory. Your job is simply to find the marbles! When you work a territory for the first time, remember that your names and your knowledge of that specific area will serve you more than almost any other factor. If you aren't immediately successful, you might be tempted to start working elsewhere. Remember, that means you'll be starting from scratch and will need to establish yourself in that new area where you have no pre-approach, have no names, and they know nothing about you.

Working your new area in a circuit deserves more detail. As a rule, in direct sales, you'll find that people are home in three major shifts:

1) During the day (8am-3pm)—Moms and dads who either stay at home or work from home, retirees, unemployed, college kids, and so on
2) Early afternoon (3pm-5pm)—Mainly parents bringing kids home from school, folks between shifts, or some that get off work a little early
3) Early evening (5pm-10pm)—The largest force of people getting home from work, older kids returning from school activities, and families getting together back at the house

Looking at this overview, if you're working a new area, your goal is to map your area through the first periods of the day. Get as much pre-approach as you can, and you might even get into some doors and make some sales during this process. Look at this like a video game. Get as much info as you can as quickly as you can. Once you get to 3pm, simply head back to where you began the day mapping and look for houses that have "life" (it's apparent that someone is home). Pop over to those houses to either sell them or cross them off the list.

Continue to go back over your map, setting evening appointments, getting more detailed pre-approach, and, hopefully, some sales, and continue until 5pm. Then, repeat the process a third time, only diverting to see appointments that you'd set up throughout the day or referrals that you'd been sent to see. As the days of the week go by, continue to add to your map, following this same system, but keeping an eye out for those "signs of life" on those earlier houses so that you can cross them off.

Going back and ensuring that you've seen every house is what we call "working tight." Always work your territory tight to make sure that you haven't missed anyone, but more important, those missing houses will be the *easiest* for you to call on because you'll know the names of all their neighbors and probably a lot more about them as well. Why call on a house that you know nothing about when you have such a warm lead to go after?

Leads

In some instances, you're going to have the opportunity to get leads, either through your company, or from outside vendors. Some companies will give these to you at no cost, but this is far less common than most companies that will either charge you for the leads that they supply you, or have you work through vendors. In either case, leads can be a valuable way to get you in the door with a new prospective client, but just like everything else, it's always based on YOU and your drive to contact as many of those leads in the most effective way possible.

Dialing

When following up on any type of lead list, you want to track your numbers to start to understand the true cost of each lead. For example, lets say that over the course of the day you work on a list of 30 leads. First off, you should work your phone list in much the same fashion that you'd work in a door to door neighborhood:

1) Call through your list once at the beginning of the day. This is a great opportunity to catch folks that work a later shift or might be home makers.
2) Call through your list a second time in the afternoon. Lunch breaks and brining the kids home from school will be breaks from the normal workday.
3) Call a third time in the evening. This is stereotypically the best time to call and set appointments, because most workers are getting back home around 5pm.

Through those calling times, you should be tracking:

1) The amount of calls you've made
2) The number of appointments you've set up
3) The outcome of those appointments (i.e. presentation with sale vs no sale, etc.)

By tracking these numbers, you'll start to find ratios that you can use in determining your success. For example:

maybe you find that for every 5 calls you make, you'll get someone to answer the phone...

and for every 5 people that answer the phone, you set an appointment

and you have a show rate of 60% when you set appointments

then you track that your closing ratio is 50% for every appointment that you present to

and that your average commission earned (or product amount sold) is "X" per client

What these factors allow you to do is create your own salary as a commissioned agent. Commit to making the number of calls that will subsequently lead to the sales numbers you're looking to achieve for that week / month / year. We call this "reverse engineering" of your numbers. By simply working backwards from your commission or sales goal, you can discover the activity that you need to be doing to achieve that goal! The great thing is that the more practiced you become within each of these areas, your success rates will go up, and your results will reflect that!

Mystery Messages

When dialing on leads, the question arises as to; Should you leave a message? What should that message be? When do I give up on a lead? There are no "right answers," but there are some techniques that we know will make a difference in your calls. One of these methods is what we call a mystery message. This type of message gives the prospect enough information to pique some interest into who called them, to in most cases call you back. In this example, notice how basic these calls really are:

"Hey Dan, it's Stephanie! Your brother, Brian mentioned this was probably the best time of day to catch you, sorry we missed each other. I should be free between 2 and 3, please ring me back then, Thanks!"

Notice that:

Stephanie didn't say why she was calling

She didn't state what company she worked for

She DID mention his brother, Brian, so he knows there's a connection to his family

Double Dialing

Another powerful method as your dialing is to call twice immediately. Instead of leaving a message after your first attempt, hang up and immediately dial your prospect back. Usually people don't call back to back unless it's important, and your call is definitely important. If you don't reach them the 2nd time, leave them a mystery message, or a message expressing the importance of their return call, and repeat the process in your next period later on that day.

Setting Solid Phone Appointments

When calling leads, there are some amazing tools at your disposal to help solidify appointments, and increase your show rate. Now first off, YES, people will set appointments with you and NOT show up. We call this "ghosting," and it's more prevalent that you think. If you're like most of your counterparts, you'll struggle with not understanding why this great person you booked the appointment with has suddenly disappeared but take solace in the fact that you're not the only one! This is incredibly common, but there are a few tips and tricks that can help reduce this percentage of "no-shows."

1) Meet NOW – When getting a prospect on the phone, ALWAYS try to have the appointment with them at the time that you catch them on the phone.
2) Set meetings within 24 hours. Now is the best time to meet, later today isn't as good, but still pretty good, and tomorrow the odds

of the appointment drop a little bit more. After 24 hours though, the no-show rate of appointments will stereotypically get larger and larger

   a. Send several confirmation texts for appointments that stretch out further over time
   b. Always send an immediate confirmation text of your meeting immediately after setting it

3) Ask your prospect to get a pen and paper and write your appointment down. Most of your prospects are now doing things digitally, so having them write it down on a post it, or on their desk calendar will be a visual reminder of your upcoming meeting
4) Video chat with them! This is SO effective. If you're on a phone with a video chat feature, then try and connect with them while you're talking. If you can get them to see you, and you can see them, that drastically reduces the barriers between the two of you, and they understand that they're speaking to a real human being, and you'll find that you'll get a lot more immediate meetings
5) Let them know that you're sending them a calendar invite. In most online calendars, you can add a lot to your invitation

   a. Get the clients email so you can add them
   b. Make sure to include both your names and a brief reminder of what the call is regarding
   c. Add notifications! This will make sure they're reminded (for example) 10 min, 30 min and full day, before your appointment is set
   d. Include the info on HOW you're meeting (Zoom, Microsoft Meeting, Phone Call, in person – make sure to also include location if it's in person, or WHO is initiating the all, if it's over the phone)
   e. Finally – HAVE THEM "ACCEPT" THE CALENDAR INVITE WHILE YOU'RE STILL ON THE PHONE! This makes sure that it shows up in both of your calendars, further solidifying the appointment

Chapter 6

"A good plan today is better than a perfect plan tomorrow"

General George Patton

Approach

Every part of your approach should have meaning to your prospect and shouldn't include wasted information. The approach is your first impression with the client, the first sale that you're looking to make. Remember, you're not selling your product in your approach, you're selling *you* and the idea that the prospect should spend time with you. In most transactions, the salesperson's goal should be to sit down with the prospect. Regardless of what you're selling, your chances of success are exponentially higher if you're sitting with a prospect than if you're standing at their door or talking on the phone. If you're sitting, you're selling. If you're standing, you're just talking.

A professional approach makes the prospect as comfortable as possible and gives them the information that they're most interested in. Here are some key rules of how to approach a door:

1) **Don't get in your prospect's face**. Nobody wants your nose two inches from the door when they answer it. Human nature is simple, and most people feel a sense of trespassing when you're right on

top of them. When you approach a door, ring or knock in a friendly fashion (the same knock you'd use at your best friend's mom's house), take three big steps away from the door, and turn profile to give the prospect a chance to sum you up. I'd go so far as to not even say anything or pretend you didn't realize they opened the door until they acknowledge you. This gives them a minute to realize you're not a threat.

2) **Smile and slow down.** If you're new to approaching, you'll feel rushed. It's natural. Slow down and simply smile at your prospect. Your confidence makes a huge difference here. Knowing that the outcome really doesn't matter should relieve all your stress. Your goal is simply to sit down with the prospect. If they say no, don't fret. You'll never run out of houses, so don't bank all your hopes and dreams on any one potential client.

3) **Rock onto your back heel.** This ties into #1. Especially if you're a tall guy, that little lean backward will make the prospect feel more at ease.

4) **Mirror your prospect's demeanor.** This might seem to contradict what I said earlier, but it doesn't. If you approach a door where the person answers with a baby in one arm, their keys in their hand, and a phone on their ear and they're talking quickly, make sure you mirror their speed. Always be one energy notch above them. Be a little faster and a little friendlier, but nothing beyond that or you'll come across as strange or annoying. Again, slow down if you're just starting because you'll talk a lot faster than you think.

5) **Be assumptive of the sale.** The first sale in the approach is to sit with the client, so assume that's exactly what is going to happen. Whether you're planning to sit with them outside or in their living room, visualize where that is and confidently motion to get there when the time is right in your approach. Break eye contact, wipe your feet, and if you're planning to go in, then watch them move aside for your invitation into their home.

What to Cover in an Effective Approach

1) Who are you?
2) Who are you representing?
3) Why are you there?
4) How long are you going to take?
5) Who have you been meeting with?

These five key items are vital in every approach. Most effective approaches have three parts. Part 1 is an overview of these five items, Part 2 will elaborate, and Part 3 is your "rip-cord," a last-ditch effort to try and sit with the client. At the end of all three parts, you should be asking and physically moving to try to sit with the prospect.

An Example Approach:

Part 1

> "Hi, Mrs. Jones? My name is Brian Winslow with Company X. I've been working here in Lockhart, talking to families with kids about the big summer camping extravaganza in Austin.
> I just came from Mike and Jamie Peterson's from across the street, and I was with the Garcias (next door) yesterday. I've been trying to catch you for a while.
> I apologize for being in a bit of a hurry. I only have a few minutes to give you the details. Is there a place where we can sit down?"

Part 2 (She objects or won't sit down.)

> Oh, I'm sorry. I guess you haven't heard about me yet. As I said, my name is Brian Winslow, and I work with Company X here in Lockhart.
> I know summer activities are a big deal for most folks to figure out, and you probably know many of the families that are sending their kids out to this event in June. You may know Ron and Stacy Browning, or the Jacksons, or the Bakers right up the street. Aren't their kids about the same age as yours?

Anyway, as I said, I have to catch all the parents with kids over at Anderson Elementary, so I only have a few minutes to spend with each family. Do you have a place we can sit?"

Part 3 (She still won't sit down or has another objection. Now this is a last-ditch effort to get a sale at the door.)

"So, basically, Mrs. Jones, everyone's been really excited about this event because it's run by Company X in conjunction with the Children's Museum and the Austin Fire Department. Kids learn a ton about the environment while getting a chance to interact with other children from other schools and get credit toward their next year's school curriculum."
"May I ask, have your children had an opportunity to do something like this before?"
"What similar activities have you lined up for them this summer?"
"Great! Well, if you like this, there's no cost today, and there are still openings available to guarantee a spot for all the kids. Where can we sit so I can show you some of the planned activities?"

Types of Approaches

Cold Call Approach

Let's dissect this approach—it's the most important approach to understand, because, conceptually, it ties into every other approach.

1) **Referral Approach**—Being given a referral to call on is the most powerful lead in your arsenal. A referral is given by someone to whom you've demonstrated who may or may not have bought from you; it makes no difference. The key is that they've personally recommended you to someone they know or care about.

9) **"T" or Four-Leaf-Clover Approach**—These two terms refer to what you see on a map when you look at a street of houses. For example, if you go to a referral's house and they're not home, approach the two neighbors on either side of them or the neighbor across the street. That forms the shape of a "T." If you also approach

the two neighbors that are next door to the person across the street, that resembles a four-leaf-clover.

10) **Reservice Approach**—My personal favorite and the easiest, because it's made when you return to see a client that you've already done business with.

Referral Approach

When you get a referral, try to get an address, not just a phone number. The chapter on referrals details how to achieve this goal. Your best opportunity to demo a prospect is at their front door. Focus on mentioning the name of the referrer within the first five seconds of your approach.

"Hi, Doug? I'm Brian. Did your mom, Shellie, mention that I'd be coming by to see you?"

Your prospect will immediately become more comfortable knowing that you have something in common with someone they care about, if only that you've met each other. Commonality wins!

Often, in referral sales, you don't even need to mention why you're there. Be confident and simply ask for a place to sit.

"Yeah, your mom made me promise to stop by and see you before I left town. Did I catch you in the middle of anything super important right now? Great; do you have a place where we can sit down?"

If they object, simply go to your Part 2 (second) approach to give them more information.

REMEMBER: Less is always more. You don't need to explain everything up front. Your prospect will be more inclined to hear what you have to say after you're sitting together.

A key component to the referral approach: Make sure that you're always tying in your experiences with the person that referred you to them and weave that into the different parts of the cycle of sales. In the approach, this can be as simple as mentioning some small anecdotes that you picked up or specifics about their house or hobbies:

"Yeah, Chuck was great; he mentioned that the two of you have been hunting for years."

"Your mom's kitchen remodel is amazing. Bet it's a lot different from when you were living there."

"So, Doug was telling me he's been playing phone tag with you and that "You're it!"

When working with a referral, don't limit yourself to just the person who referred you. Start to tie in anyone else with whom they might be affiliated. This might be the person who referred you to the person that referred you to the prospect. It might be other friends or relatives that you know they have in common. If you're working your referrals systematically, this will become easier and easier because you'll know so many people in their spheres of influence. These could also be people that they work with, teachers from the school, and so on. The smaller the town, the easier to connect.

"T" or Four-Leaf-Clover Approach

This approach is as close to a cold call as a veteran salesperson should ever need to do. It is what I also call my *ninja* approach, and it's one that's really fun.

Use this approach when you call on a referral or a reservice client. We'll discuss reservice later, but briefly, this is a client that you've already sold to that you're going back to see. Often, you'll drive out to see one of these clients, and they're not home. Since our primary focus is always efficiency, it would be very inefficient to drive any length of time to see someone and then drive another length of time trying to catch the next person. You can spend an entire day chasing your tail that way. You need to get in front of a prospect.

In this case, once you see that the prospect is *not* home, look for the nearest house with "life," meaning someone appears to be home. Several cars may be in the driveway. More obvious, someone's sitting out on the porch. Your job is to jog up to that location and use this version of the last approach we learned:

"Hi! I'm sorry to bother you. *Actually*, I'm not even here to see you. I'm trying to catch up with Paul and Marissa next door. Paul's brother Michael sent me over to meet with them, and they've been impossible to catch!"

"Would you mind helping me a little and let me know, is it usually better to see them around this time of day, or are evenings a little better?"

The client will answer accordingly.

"Great! (Start writing the information in your pre-approach pad.) Is there a car I should look for to know they're back, or do they normally park in the garage?"

Keep writing, and as you are, start to establish some rapport.

"By the way, I noticed the Longhorns flag on the garage. Are you folks from Austin? That's great. What brought you out here to El Paso?"

Keep politely chatting until you feel like you've connected with the prospect; then jump into an abridged version of the second approach we learned earlier.

"Oh, I'm sorry. I guess you haven't heard about me yet. My name is Brian Winslow, and I work with Company X out here in El Paso. I was with Michael earlier, and he asked me to catch up with Paul and Marissa before I left town. I really only see friends and family, so I guess you folks would qualify."

"I only have a few minutes to spend with everyone. Do you have a place to sit down?"

Here's what most likely will happen:

1) You'll get in, sit down, and demo your product.
2) You'll get a legitimately good appointment.

Some people won't let you demonstrate with them, but I promise you, if you do this right, they'll be in the minority.

And, when you finally do sit down with Paul and Marissa, you'll have another name to use, and they'll probably become clients.

This approach is fantastic because it's so efficient. You'll make more presentations, sell to more of these prospects, and open more new referral streams than you ever thought possible. Remember, the name of the game is presentations. You can't sell what you don't show, so show as often as you can.

Reservice Approach

This is fun, fun, fun, fun, fun! It's the way that sales should be, and reservicing is your reward for building a great base of clients. If you're new, you're doing all the hard work to build your "book of business" to be able to reservice. If you've been around for a while, then I hope you're selling a product or service that can handle upsells (new sales) because that's what's about to happen when you walk in.

The reservice approach is amazing because you've already overcome so many of the sales obstacles. First, you know the prospect is a buyer because ... *they've already bought from you*!!! Second, there shouldn't be any trust issues, and they're not trying to figure out who you are because ... *they've already bought from you*!!!

There is a certain order in your approach when reservicing clients. Act as though you are seeing a good friend, even if you think they might not recognize you:

"Hi, Stacy?! Remember me? It's Brian, your insurance guy from Family Heritage."

Always say your name and company to prevent them from feeling uncomfortable if they've forgotten your name or the company's name.

"Good to see you! I was back in town and needed to go over a few key items with you from your purchase. Do you have a place to sit down?"

For the approach, that's all you must do. If they object, then simply elaborate a little as to what you're going to review with them. Have this figured out ahead of time.

Once you get in, this is the outline of your visit:

1) Re-establish rapport. Reconnect with your client and get back up to speed.
2) Transition into why you stopped in and what you want to review.
3) Briefly redemonstrate the product that you previously sold them and touch base on the most valuable benefits. Get them excited about their initial purchase and compliment them on their decision to purchase it as you go through it.
4) During the demonstration, introduce your upsell item and acknowledge what both of you are already aware of: that you are going to try to sell them something new:

"You know, Brett, I wouldn't be a good sales guy if I didn't have *something* else to show you!"

1) Give them a short buying atmosphere. (There's an entire chapter on this later.)
2) Sell them on the new product.
3) *Always* get new referrals.

Chapter 7

"To be interesting, be interested"

Dale Carnegie

The Introduction: AKA Establishing Rapport and the Need

There is no more important aspect to the sales cycle than the introduction. Some might argue that the approach is the most important part because it gets you in the door, but the bottom line is this: Prospects are buying *you* as much as they're buying your product.

Let that sink in. You can do everything right in your presentation. Even if you answer every objection and dot every "i" and cross every "t," if your client doesn't like and trust you, you're going to lose most of your potential sales.

The introduction establishes rapport with a client and a means for connecting with them in some fashion that is *not* related to your product or service. It's the building of a friendship; the creation of trust. It's where comfort is born between you and your prospect. Now, you also establish *need* in the introduction, but we'll get to that later.

The introduction occurs either immediately after the approach or when you first connect with the client after a scheduled appointment. Your immediate goal in this situation is to spend at least five to ten minutes discussing *anything—except* what you're trying to pitch. This is your time to get to know your prospect, and their time to get to know you. If you immediately began talking about what you're selling, there'd be no foundation to build on, which would almost certainly lead to procrastination issues at the end of your presentation.

Procrastination is tied to the prospect's lack of trust about you and your product:

"You know what? Let me do a little more research and get back to you."
"We never make a snap decision; let's follow up in a couple of weeks."
"Why don't you leave me your paperwork and a copy of the agreement so I can have my lawyer go over it?"

Control the Environment
When you walk into a place where you're going to present, that is *your* space for the time that you're there. That means, take control of your area. If you're in someone's living room, direct them where to sit so that you'll be able to demonstrate comfortably. If their TV is blaring, let them know how your attention span is horrible around a TV, and is it okay if you turn it down (and then turn it off!). If the kids are running around like crazy, find a way to politely get them off to another room.

In an office, the same rules apply. If possible, to make things more casual and free, ask your prospects to come out and sit with you in the chairs in front of the desk. If you're making a group presentation, direct the managers on what you need to make the best use of their time. Don't let them direct you in how to present. They don't know your business.

Relationship Building 101
Building a relationship with your client is the most important facet of the entire sales process; therefore, focus your time and energy on the introduction. How do you build good rapport with a prospect that you haven't met?

First, be strategic with your questions and follow some simple guidelines. Second, use the environment to your advantage. Last, adhere to the 90/10 rule, which simply is that when you start building rapport, have the prospect speak at least 90% of the time.

Strategy and Guidelines

Regardless of the nature of your product or service, building a referral base is a proven way to expand your business. This is true in nearly every direct sales opportunity. Don't wait until the end of the sale to get referrals. It's awkward to finish up by asking for referrals as you exit. This *can* be effective, but often you'll hear, "I really don't know a lot of people" or "I can't think of anyone that would need X service." By asking questions during the introduction, you can obtain numerous referral names just by asking the questions that they'd love to brag about:

"Karen, are you folks originally from here, or did you move from somewhere else?"

"Do you have a big family?"

"Do your brothers and sisters all live here in McAllen?"

"Where do you work? What do you do there? How many people do you manage?"

"How long have you been on the PTA/PTO? How many members do you have?"

"Do you go to Fourth Street Presbyterian Church? Are you very involved?"

These ideas will open a dialogue between you and the prospect. Remember who people *love* to talk about? *Themselves!* This is their chance to shine, so let them. This is a surefire way to create a connection and get a running start on referrals.

Names

Having prospects share names with you is key, but using names with your referrals is even more important. You can do this in different ways:

First, if you're new to an area, do your research, much of which you can do via the Internet. Read the local newspaper to see what people are talking about. What are the area schools? What's the high school mascot? What is the town known for: oil and gas, tech companies, farming? For which local companies might your prospects likely work? Do your research to become a part of your territory.

After you've started to work an area, share the stories of the people whom you've already met or worked with. Working your referrals systematically is incredibly powerful because your prospects are sure to know many of the folks with whom you've spoken, and this makes you immediately more trustworthy because you're a part of the community. Don't just drop names, elaborate and share stories. Look for names that create a sparkle in your prospect's eye. When you detect that recognition, share items to deepen the connection between you and your new prospect:

"Oh, do you know the Parkers? Yeah, they're fantastic! I was over with Peter and Jen last week. Did you see the new pool they're building in the back yard for the kids? It's amazing! Peter is doing a lot of the patio work himself, and Jen was laughing because she said she'd never even seen him hold a hammer!"

These little stories create community between you and your prospects. They show that you're not just some solicitor, you're a staple in the community, and people are taking the time to hear what you have to say. The tighter that you work an area, the stronger your names become.

Unwise Topics

As guidelines go, this may be a tough one for you, but it's great advice that you've heard before. Do *not* take a stand on religion or politics. Notice I *didn't* say "do not talk" about these, because you may not have a choice, but I urge you not to get ensnared in a debate, even if you hold strong views to the contrary. Now, if you're reading this book, and your sale *is* religion or politics, then obviously you will need to share your views at a certain point, but don't do it in the introduction. Let this be their opportunity to say what they need to and express their thoughts. Remember, at the end of the day, you're not trying to win every battle; you're trying to win the war! Keep the end goal in mind, always.

Use the Environment

If you're in someone's home or office, you can't miss their display of trophies or pictures that are important to them in some way. Think about your own living room or office. Don't you show off things that have meaning? Look for those items and see where you might be able to connect, or at least pay them a compliment that will get them to open up. For example:

- You might have a sports team in common, or at least a decent rivalry between your two teams.
- Perhaps they love to hunt.
- You might have kids or grandkids around the same ages as the ones you see in the pictures.
- Maybe some displayed books are books that you've also read.
- Look for any connection.

The Spouse

When it comes to environment, make sure to get all the "players" in front of you. If you're sitting with Mrs. Jones, and Mr. Jones is in another room or out mowing, get him in. She says he won't be interested? *Go get him anyway*! This may seem uncomfortable, but I promise you that you can't find a better use of your time. Be lighthearted, smile a lot, but jog out to that mower, wave him down, and let him know what's going on:

"Hey, Paul! I'm meeting with Jeanette inside, going over some stuff for your family, and I wanted to grab you quickly to give you a break from the yard. Is it easier for you if we meet with you out here on the patio or inside at the kitchen table?" (Remember to always give two positive options.)

If you don't go through the process of getting the spouse, then you risk the very real possibility that once you're done presenting, Mrs. Jones will say, "This sounds good, but let me run it by my husband."

The result being, you're depending on her to give him an abridged version of the sales talk that you just gave her. What are the odds she's going to make a presentation that's even a fraction as good as the one you've been perfecting? She can't!

Always work to get that spouse to the table.

Unpeeling the Layers

When you're asking these questions, you may run into the prospect who says, "Can we just get to the point?" or "I don't have a lot of time; just give me your pitch." Always acknowledge their objection but continue to work toward creating connection. Find a way to circle back to questions that will get them to open up to you and create a relationship. Humor is a good tool, but, at the very least, get them excited to talk about something that they obviously love.

Once you get them talking, go into depth about what they're sharing. Use your questions to dig deeper into their answers. A good rule of thumb is the rule of three. Ask three follow-up questions that will open them up to you. Find out more about their spheres of influence, the things that they enjoy, their connections in the community. This will begin to build trust and build the foundation of your business relationship through friendship.

Never Split the Difference

In Chris Voss's critically acclaimed book on negotiation, he speaks about the power of mirroring. He uses the term differently than I do in this book, but what he suggests is taking two or three words from what your prospect has just said and repeating that to them in an inquisitive way. For example, if your client tells you they recently moved to the area and are now working at the local engineering plant, you might ask, "The local plant?" which, in turn, might encourage them to elaborate by speaking about their duties and how they've been put into a managerial role.

Follow up with, "A managerial role?"

This leads them to further elaborate that they manage fifteen of the plant workers and perhaps what their responsibilities are.

This simple form of getting clients to elaborate is extremely effective and noninvasive to the client. It not only forms a bond for you with the client, but it has also, in this example, opened the possibility of fifteen new referrals that you can call on in the future.

Establishing a Connection
After you've established that connection, start revealing why your product or service might be good for them. I personally have sold everything from educational books to insurance, and when I transition into selling my insurance products, I generally ask a question to start establishing the importance of my product to the prospect.

"Well, as I said, Jeanette, I've been working out here talking to everyone about cancer. I know it's not a fun topic to talk about, but it sure seems to affect a lot of people in this area. If you don't mind my asking, who is the closest person that you know who's been affected by cancer?"

Those powerful lines allow me to comfortably transition from whatever we were discussing to cancer without it being out of the blue. I engage them in what they need to be thinking about, and they start giving me key points that I'll use later in my presentation. The more you get your prospects on the same page with you, the better. This process takes them back to a time when they struggled (emotionally or financially) with someone that they cared about.

By continuing to ask follow-up questions, I also learn if the person survived. How long did they fight the disease? Did they have to travel? Did they help financially? I'm asking these probing questions incredibly "softly" and very respectfully. For this product, the questions are very personal and bring back some hard memories. That's what you want!

People must remember the pain. They need to remember how hard it was paying the bills or dealing with finding someone to watch the kids. They have to go back to when they were skipping work to take their wife to chemo treatments, or how they lost two incomes when they both had to stop working because they had a child being treated. People forget those things on purpose because it's painful. Our job is to stop them from re-experiencing those financial hardships, so they often need to remember their past pain to understand the importance of what I'm offering.

Now, *establishing* the need and *finding* the need are two different things. In the previous example, if a family has dealt with cancer firsthand, then the need should be easily established. On the other hand, how do you work with a prospect who doesn't know anyone who's had cancer, and they really don't see the need? Find a need.

You can find a need in various ways, although I think statistics are most effective with stories.

"One out of two men and one out of three women will get cancer, so…."

"The number one cause of death for people under the age of 70 is accidents."

"The burglary rate in your city has gone up by 30% in the past two years."

Statistics are even more powerful when used in conjunction with local stories and are even more powerful when you can use names or testimonials. Whether you're establishing or finding the need, begin to weave together information that you've learned from the introduction and some of the names and statistics that you want to share. This combination builds trust and curiosity. Ultimately, it should lead them to the realization that they have an issue that may need solving—and that you might be the person to provide a solution.

Framing and Conviction

Whatever you're selling, there must be compelling reasons for your prospect to purchase. *You* must know what those reasons are before they do. The gist of framing is that when two people approach a situation, they see the situation from their unique perspectives (aka their "frames"). Imagine this as the different lenses through which we view life. For example, if you've been cheated in business, you'll probably be more jaded in viewing future partnerships than someone who's had successful business dealings.

When working with a prospect, your conviction and belief in your product must go beyond how much you love it. Ask yourself, "Why is this something that is a no-brainer for my prospect?" This is *so* vitally important to your presentation, because it allows you to be empathetic to their issues, while not becoming sympathetic and having them talk you out of why they should move forward in the sale.

Sympathy is your understanding of why a prospect just can't afford it right now or can't decide, and you are totally with them. Heck, if you were in the same situation, you don't know how you'd get by either!

Empathy is your understanding of why a prospect just can't afford it right now or can't make a decision, and your realization that if they don't get what you have, that could put them in an even worse scenario.

For example, you're an alarm salesperson and a prospect laments that times are tough, and they're barely making it day to day. Their spouse was just laid off, and both breadwinners might be on the brink of losing their jobs. That's a tough situation, but let's review what your mental process might be:

a) My product can prevent a robbery or burglary, saving them from a theft that might ruin them overnight or even lead to the harm or death of one of their family members.

b) Their neighborhood has had a major uptick in robberies and home invasions.

c) My product will substantially bring down their homeowners' insurance, actually saving money in the long run.

So now, the idea of framing takes shape. Understand that *the person with the stronger frame will win. Always.*

This doesn't mean that the prospect will always buy, but there is *always* a sale made during an objection. Either they sell you on their objections (usually price or procrastination), or you sell them on why your product or service is so important. When you are 100% convinced about the value of your product and understand why your product is important for them to have, then when you get an objection, your initial reaction will be to help them understand those benefits, as opposed to feeling sympathetic (weaker frame) and walking away from the encounter.

Framing begins in your approach, where your conviction about why you should sit down with a prospect takes root. You see it in top salespeople, and I can't think of any successful person in any endeavor that doesn't have conviction to a giant degree. Now understand that if you use this with a product or service that you don't believe in, it changes from an important piece of your sales process to manipulation, and if that's your goal, please close this book and move on. The point is that conviction is the major component of establishing or creating the need.

A Strong Buildup
Statistics garner attention, but your prospect must understand why your product or service is different and necessary. Later, when you get into the demonstration, you'll start to show the meat of what you're selling but remember that people don't purchase because of the meat. "Sell the sizzle; *not* the steak." No kid is as excited about a Christmas gift after they open it, as they were seeing that big package sitting for weeks under the tree.

Most car owners don't care about the inner workings of the engine or the air conditioning system, they just care that the car is sexy, powerful, or safe. Zig Ziglar famously said that "Sales is a transference of emotion." From that, we derive that it's *not* a transference of logic. When a prospect buys from you, it's because what you're selling is going to leave them with a specific feeling, not necessarily because of the details of what makes your product great.

With this understanding, your buildup should center on making the client feel what your product will ultimately deliver for them. If you're selling alarms, it may be peace of mind or safety. If it's a new house, it may be prestige or growth. If it's insurance, it might be financial security. Whatever it is, they need to understand that there is a gap in what they have, and you have the ability to fill that gap with the best possible solution, *but* they have to come to that conclusion based on the journey that you take them on through your presentation.

Chapter 7

Hopefully, if you're working for a professional organization, you have a scripted presentation that will walk you through the sales cycle and explain each step, but if not, or if you own a company and are developing this for your sales staff, then let me share what I currently do through my insurance brokerages:

1. After explaining the statistics of how devastating cancer can be (one of two men, one of three women, and three of four families will experience cancer), I transition into how over a million new cases will be diagnosed in the U.S. this year.
2. That leads to showing that although there are some hereditary cancers, over 75% come from environmental factors.
3. Then I relay that forty years ago, a cancer diagnosis usually led to death. The *great* news, though, is that today, most (over 60%, in fact) will survive *but*—in surviving, they can incur additional expenses that, in some cases, drag on for years. Besides the normal doctor and hospital bills are costs that health insurance *doesn't* pay for. How do you pay those bills, *especially* if you no longer work?
4. I ask them to list additional costs that would impact this issue: rent, mortgage, utilities, insurance premiums, childcare, travel, gas, food.... The list goes on and on.
5. We offer the Series 6-Plus plans that do X, Y, and Z.

By this time, they should really be "with me," and if they're not, I need to work harder before I go forward. If they're not emotionally connected now, they won't be when I move from the sizzle to the steak. So how do we gauge if we should move forward?

Yes Questions (Again!)

As you start establishing the need, ask questions that gauge the temperature of your client. Two primary types of questions establish landmarks that guide you through your demo.

Simple Assumptive Questions—Throw these in whenever you point out something significant. Follow up the significant item(s) with phrases such as, "Isn't that great?" "Can you see why everyone has been getting this from me?" "Can you believe they include that?"

As you're asking, keep eye contact with your prospect and nod your head to provide the audio and visual stimulation to encourage agreement. Also, yes questions get the client used to saying the word "yes." For example, rapidly say "pop, stop, and drop" three times; then immediately answer the question: "What do you do at a green light?"

Admit it: You said, "Stop;" obviously wrong. You *go* at a green light. We love patterns, and we get in the habit of following them. Asking yes questions is no different.

Choose Questions from Two Positives—The other type of yes question lets the prospect choose from two positives. Use these to transition from your demo to your price buildup and into your close. Ask what the prospect likes most about your product or service: "the fact that the knives never need sharpening" or "the fact that a lifetime warranty allows returns forever, no questions asked?" The answer can be one, the other, or both. In most cases they won't look for the unoffered "I don't like anything" response.

No Questions

Ironically, these can be as effective as the yes questions, and with certain clients, an even more effective sales technique. Either technique works if used correctly.

"No" is powerful because it's what we generally feel most comfortable with in our day-to-day lives. The word no doesn't commit us to anything. It doesn't put us on the line. It gets us out of situations we don't want to be in. It's our "safe-word." If you're working with a standoffish prospect who doesn't seem to be in tune with your presentation, this is the place to use no questions.

So, how do you frame a no question? Simply find a way to ask a yes question that substitutes no as the positive response:

"Aren't those benefits amazing? "*Yes.*"

"Would you be opposed to getting something that has these types of benefits?" "*No.*"

Chapter 8

"All Battles are fought by scared men who would rather be somewhere else"

Captain Rockwell ("Rock") Torrey

The Buying Atmosphere

We enter a powerful portion of the sales process. Most salespeople can't close on a single visit, and most believe that multiple visits are a prerequisite of any sales call. I'm here to tell you that in most cases, you'll never excel in your field if you don't set up your sales to be decided that day.

Don't get me wrong, if you're selling jets or yachts or doing business to business (B2B) sales that might require several gatekeepers, multiple visits might be necessary. I assure you that plenty of jets, yachts, and B2B sales have also closed in one visit. Don't convince yourself that it's not possible.

The buying atmosphere is established prior to the presentation of the benefits (meat) of your product or service. Your prospect learns how you do business and that this is their opportunity to window shop. If they're on the fence about the product, it's perfectly reasonable for them to say no, and, frankly, you'd prefer they do that, because you don't want them to get something they're not 100% sold on, *but*, if they do like what you have, it's super easy to get them signed up, and it only takes a few minutes. Since you have limited time to spend with everyone, you can sit down with them just *once*.

"All I ask is, just give me a thumbs up or down after I show you? Is that fair? Great."

The buying atmosphere creates a promise from the buyer to you, and vice versa:

   a) They're going to give you a definitive yes or no today.
   b) You're going to be 100% satisfied with either decision.

This is a vital part of your overall demonstration because it lets the prospect know that they're expected to decide when you wrap up, as opposed to this being the first of multiple appointments.

I'd love to report that your clients will fully understand and will never go back on this promise. The reality is that procrastination is human nature. They do it, I do it, and you do it. It's just part of who we are.
Prospects will look at you and say:

"Dan, I have to be honest. I didn't expect to love this as much as I did, but:

"I don't make decisions on the spot."
"I need to talk with my wife."
"I have to pray on it."

These are normal responses, even if you've created a great buying atmosphere. Remember, though, that how you respond is what transforms you from a professional presenter to a professional salesperson. If you get no objections, you've presented something that they'll probably buy. Your skill comes into play when you successfully counteract objections, so don't fear them, get to them as quickly as possible and hone your craft.

Never Go Back

Why do a one-visit close? Why don't you give people time to think about it? These are good questions asked frequently by new salespeople. Their first reaction is that it feels manipulative, as if we're rushing clients and not giving them time to think. Never go back is one of the most important concepts in this book and in your selling career, and one I want to make very clear:

Prospects do not think or get more excited about your product after you leave.

As a salesperson, your job is to show your product or service as often as you can. The law of averages or law of large numbers stipulates that if you have a good offering and see a good number of people, a certain percentage of people will buy.

Bottom line: The better the product or service and the more practiced and professional your presentation, the faster your sales will increase. Most prospects won't want to decide, so instead of them giving you a yes or a no, they'll give you a maybe. If they're a no, don't waste your time. You promised you'd be okay with a no.

If they're a maybe, this is where the real sale begins, and we'll get into that when we discuss the rebuttal system. At this point, remember that your *frame* needs to be stronger than theirs. Mrs. Jones is a good saleswoman. She'll sell you on why she's going to get it; she just needs to talk to her husband, compare your product to something else, or whatever. Unless you don't accept returns and have no cancellation policy of any kind, her objection is something you must overcome. Remember, don't get sold by her, because she's good!

When creating a buying atmosphere, keep it simple. Don't create doubt in the mind of your prospect. If you keep hammering that they must decide today, they may become convinced that they *must* take time to think about it. You created the objection for them.

If the prospect understands that there's a decision to be made and that you're okay with either decision, then you've created the proper buying atmosphere. Now, family and friends? That's entirely different.

The Buying Atmosphere for Family and Friends

Here's the challenge: Family and friends will take advantage of you. You can create the buying atmosphere, yet they'll come back with a ton of objections. My favorite is:

"What? If I see you in three weeks and want to get it, you're not going to sell it to me?"

So how do we deal with this? The key is to *pound* your buying atmosphere. Don't do this with a general client but *do it* with family and friends. Basically, the buying atmosphere reads the same as I shared above, but after you go through the entire presentation, follow up by saying something like this:

"Is that fair? Listen, Brian, I want to make sure you get this: I'm your friend; not your salesperson. I'm only going to be your salesperson for the next little bit, so just understand, once I show this to you, I'm done being a sales guy with you, okay? That means we'll either get you signed up today, or we won't talk about it again. I promise, if you love it, we'll figure something out, but what I'm not okay with is me calling you a few days from now, and you looking at your phone and seeing it's me, and sending me to voicemail because you think I'm probably calling to see if you want to buy. You understand, right? Great!"

I always add this additional bit, and I always laugh about it, and they laugh back because they know that's exactly what would happen if I called. They still may object at the end, but because I laid the foundation, it allows me to leave the presentation with a sale or the comfort that we won't be revisiting the discussion. Don't become a professional appointment setter, especially with the people you're closest with.

Chapter 9

"There is nothing either good or bad, but thinking makes it so"

William Shakespeare

The Demonstration

Believe it or not, this is the *least* important part of your presentation. Unless you're selling a highly technical product with very specific needs for your client's problem, they're not going to care much about the "meat" of your product. "Sell the sizzle, not the steak" applies here.

Car buyers don't care about the brand of sparkplugs, the type of Freon in the AC, transmission details, or the fact that the seats have double stitching. They care that the car is safe, looks good, and is reliable. If you ask most people what's important to them in a car, you might get similar responses:

- It fits their entire family
- It gets great gas mileage
- It's environmentally friendly
- It's fast
- It looks great

This is true with most products and services. Your work in leading up to the demo should establish the reasons why they need what you have.

Hopefully, you've already piqued their interest in buying. The demo gives them a few *relevant* things to tie everything together.

The purpose of the demo is to get the client above the buying line, so you can move into the close.

The Buying Line

The buying line is the point at which a prospect's interest has risen to the level that they're ready to be closed. They won't necessarily buy, but you must recognize when they reach this point, because it will give you the greatest amount of time and opportunity to close the sale.

Legend:
1. Get them Interested
2. Close!
3. They're losing interest
4. Too late...

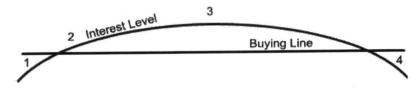

The graph illustrates that, as you're going through your presentation, your prospect's interest should gradually rise. This doesn't necessarily happen during the demonstration, but it's generally here where people feel most comfortable moving into the close. Oftentimes, you'll find the prospect's interest level rising very early in your presentation, and they'll start to ask questions that lead you to recognize this state. These are called buying questions.

"How much does this cost?"
"Do you give discounts if I buy more than one?"
"How long did you say my neighbors have owned this?"
"What's the warranty?"
"Is there a contract?"

Chapter 9

If you get these questions early, that's great! So, what do you do? CLOSE!! Alec Baldwin made this clear in the classic movie *Glengarry Glen Ross*: "Always Be Closing!"

Another indicator is when a prospect gets that glimmer in their eye. This comes with time, but we all look for these signs in everyday life, so it should come rather naturally. If you're dating someone new, that glimmer is when you feel it's safe to lean in for that first kiss. If you're a teen, that glimmer might be during a conversation with your dad that indicates that the is right time to ask to borrow the car.

Yes Questions (This keeps coming up for a reason!)

Remember that in sales, we get a chance to gauge the temperature of our clients by asking yes questions. "Yes," questions are generally filler questions to make sure that your client is with you and staying engaged in the presentation. They keep your presentation from becoming a monologue, and they require engagement by your prospect.

"Can you see why everyone's been getting this from me?"

"Isn't that great?"

"Wouldn't this have made a huge difference if your aunt had had this?"

To gauge temperature, it's not just them answering, "Yes," it's deciphering *how* they say it. If they're monotone, then follow up with a question to get them more fully engaged. Questions will always be your go-to in a sales scenario. They help you figure out where your prospect is and where you need to focus during your presentation.

NOTE: DON'T BE AFRAID TO ASK QUESTIONS, and *don't answer for your clients!* This is another common occurrence that you see in even veteran sales reps. Many reps try to fill voids with their own voices to eliminate the opportunity for objections. This is the exact *opposite* of how you should be thinking. Yearn for objections! Get them early so you can address them. Let your clients open up to you and learn how to get them to do it. Otherwise, they'll be thinking about their objection through your entire presentation, and they won't *hear* you anyway. They'll be listening, but not hearing. Here's an example.

Early in my insurance career selling to military families, I didn't know about military insurance. Instead of listening to objections, I'd rush through my demo. I knew that we had a great product, and if I could only tell them everything, that would erase any of their concerns. *Wrong*!

They'd politely sit there, and during the close, I'd hear:

"Dan, this looks like a great product, and I can see why so many people would get it, but we just don't need it because we have Tri-Care."

Military families became one of my biggest niches when I finally began anticipating this objection early. Instead of them just waiting to shoot me down, they learned that we could fill gaps in their coverage and extend other benefits.

With all that being said, when you gauge your prospect's temperature, you sense when they're really with you and they understand *why* what you're selling is so important.

This stage indicates that someone has gone from Level 1 on our graph to Level 2. Their interest has risen above the buying line, and they're ready to move to the purchase. Now, this doesn't mean that they're going to just roll over and sign up with you, but it does mean that they've seen enough to start the process.

When a prospect rises above the line, transition to the price buildup and close as soon as possible. In most closing situations, you may need to answer objections or close again, even multiple times. The earlier you start this process, the more time you'll have before the prospect slips below the buying line.

YOUR AVERAGE SALESPERSON

The most common thing that a new salesperson does is show too much before getting to the close. This is for two reasons:

1) They're nervous and anxious to close the deal.
2) They're excited that the prospect is excited, and they want to show them more and more to retain that feeling.

The second is the most common, because it's fun to show off your product or service. We all love being the life of the party, and this is basically what you've become if you have passion for your product, and you're showing it the right way. The problem is that as you're showing more and more benefits, your prospect is moving farther and farther across that buying line. At a certain point, their responses aren't as strong as they were just a bit earlier, and you realize they've passed Number 3 on the graph. They're still willing to purchase, but their interest is waning, and you're racing time before they fall below the line.

When a prospect falls below the line, it's virtually impossible to get them back, so close early and close often. If you can't close the sale before they drop below the line, tuck your tail between your legs, salvage your time by getting some strong referrals, and move on.

KEEP SOME BULLETS IN YOUR GUN

We've established that the demonstration is the least important part of the cycle of sales, but let's also acknowledge that the demonstration is the one that you'll fall back on when dealing with rebuttals. Although this will be a later chapter, it ties heavily into the concept of leaving some of your best benefits out of your demonstration when you initially present to the prospect.

Most salespeople struggle with this concept, but let me challenge you with this:

It's better to have your best benefits available to show to get someone RE-excited, versus when you're early in the presentation and they're already excited.

When you begin your demonstration, share just enough of the benefits to prove that your product or service does what you've been saying that it does. You found a need in their life, and you have something to help fill that need. Now you've shown how your offering can do it. That doesn't mean that you should reveal everything.

When you get rebuttals, be prepared with your best benefits. Get them re-engaged on *why* they wanted to buy. For that reason, you shouldn't just have bullets, you should have cannon fire! Have a bazooka-style benefit waiting for them that they're going to get really excited about so you can re-close and walk away with the sale.

MULTIPLE PRODUCTS

If you're selling more than one product or showing different lines of products that you think your prospect should buy, first ask yourself, "Do these additional products or lines work fundamentally the same way, or substantially different?"

This is important because if they're substantially different, incorporate that information *prior* to the buying atmosphere. If they work fundamentally the same, quickly explain those additional products and effectively add them to your final package.

For example, if you're selling alarm systems, your pitch deals with the overall safety of the household. By the time you've reached the demonstration, you've established that they not only need an alarm to keep out intruders, they also need protection from carbon monoxide poisoning, fire, or even their children leaving the house in the middle of the night.

After you've demonstrated your main product and deduced that they've gone above the buying line, simply summarize these other great bundled services. Even though your demo was focused on the alarm and monitoring services, the extra two minutes you spend quickly touching on these side services lets you expand your pricing range to the clients. We'll explore the value in laying this groundwork in the next chapter.

FINAL TRANSITION

During the demo when you're ready to move to the price buildup, you need a powerful transition. It must be thought out and a little weightier than your yes questions. This should be a yes or yes question, as covered earlier, and will empower you to go through the price and then the close:

"Mrs. Jones, I'm just curious. From what you've seen so far, what do you like most about the product or service, the fact that it does X or because it does Y?"

"Yeah, there's no correct answer. I was just curious about what appealed most to you. I'm sure you're wondering what this costs, right?"

Move on to the price buildup.

Chapter 10

"Money is not the prime asset in life. Time is"

Gordon Gekko, Wall Street: Money Never Sleeps

The Price Buildup

ASSIGNING VALUE

The first thing that any prospect should know is the value of your product or service. You could be selling magazines, books, alarms, insurance, cleaner, religion, a political candidate, really anything, and the client is going to be thinking about what this might cost. In my last two examples, value would be based on the alternative. What's the cost of atheism? What's the cost if the other person wins? With products, if *you* don't sell them on a value, then *they* will assign one for themselves.

For example, if you're selling knives, I might immediately associate the value of your knives with the knives I last purchased. Maybe I bought them online or at a discount shop. If you don't sell me on the value of your knives, and I spent $150 on my last set, your $900 "deal" might completely turn me off to anything else you have to say.

On the flip side, there are some features that might interest the buyer:

- The knives were crafted in Japan at an ancient monastery by the same monks that have made swords for the Samurai for the past 3,000 years.

- An average sword that they sell goes for over $15K per sword.
- These same knives are used by chefs in over 90% of the top-rated restaurants in the world.
- Oh, by the way, those restaurant knives generally sell for over $300 each and have a three- year waiting list, so this 12-knife set is valued at over $3,000, *if* you can get them.
- There's a small allotment manufactured exclusively for the U.S. market, and instead of having to wait *and* pay that same rate, the same set is available to you for *only* $900!

Here's the thing: It's still the same set of knives as in the first example, the difference being that instead of just blurting out a price, an effective price buildup in the second example showed the buyer the value of their purchase.

THE POWER OF INFOMERCIALS

If you watch TV past the midnight hour or if you're a fan of Home Shopping Network or QVC, you're bombarded with infomercials. Ginsu knives, food dehydrators, ShamWow cloths, and Orange Glo are just a few of the thousands of items that are sold daily though your television screen. The common element in every one of these products is a solid price buildup and usually a strong call to action that pushes you to an immediate buying decision.

In insurance, we use the same concepts in assigning value. My company sells supplemental cancer plans that pay directly into personal accounts if a client is diagnosed with cancer, *but* if they don't use the plan, their premiums are refunded at a future maturity date. It gives protection when they need it, and when they don't, they've basically just stuck their money in a safe deposit box for those years. Here's our price buildup, picking up from where we left off in the last chapter:

"So, Mrs. Jones, I'm sure you're wondering about the expense. It must be costly with all these benefits, right?

Many people assume that a product like this costs around the same as health insurance because of the catastrophic nature of what it covers and the fact that the cash comes to *you*. Right now, if you bought healthcare privately for you, your husband, and your kids, you'd probably be looking at around $1,000, right?

You might think that a plan like this runs about $1,000 or more for a family of five because, well, first, your health insurance plan won't send *you* a check if you contract cancer. Their job is to pay the doctors and the hospitals. We'll pay everything to you *directly* because who knows your bills better than you and your husband? Nobody!

The second reason people assume that this is a $1,000 plus plan for a family your size is because you must pay that $7,100 deductible you mentioned before your plan pays *anybody anything*! Our plan pays you on the *first* eligible dollar you claim, and, in many cases, it will pay you with *no limits*. You can even use that money toward your deductibles.

Probably the biggest reason, Mrs. Jones, that people assume this plan is at that $1,000+ level is because, believe it or not, you can file as many claims on this plan as you like, and you can get as old as you're going to get. We have *never* raised our rates even one dollar. This applies no matter how many claims you file or what your age becomes.

Here's the great thing. Instead of being at that $1,000+ rate, this plan to cover you, your husband and *all* three kids is only $85 for the *entire* family! And that includes the Intensive Care Plan. Isn't that amazing?!"

At this point, I must become super intuitive again, but let's put that off for just a second. I want to emphasize some of the nuances in the psychology of how we present this price buildup.

REPEAT THE VALUE

Notice that through this price buildup, I repeated the "$1,000+" cost several times. This is by design. You want them to appreciate the value of what you're selling, and you want to remind them of the cost of something else that they're either paying for or are very aware of, so in this case, remind them again and again that their health insurance would be over $1,000.

Additionally, I didn't assign value by just throwing out one thing to compare to. In this case, I gave them three distinct examples:

a) Their health insurance doesn't pay *them*. We do.
b) Their health plan makes them pay out of pocket *first* for deductibles and copays. We don't.
c) Their health insurance costs increase or change based on their usage or age. Ours won't.

This process is powerful and assigns value.

ESTIMATE COST ASSUMPTIVELY

In any industry, know about the products you're comparing. In the preceding case, I was comparing to health insurance and assumptively told the prospects that their cost might be over $1,000 for a family of five. I know this because I know my industry. Are there programs that are lower than that? Possibly, but generally, those would be base-bottom plans that have the minimum limits of coverage, and even then, they're not much cheaper. Healthcare costs are a travesty in today's market.

The family could have countered that they have insurance through work, so they only pay $200 a month, or some crazy amount. When I phrased the question, however, I specifically asked, "If you were to get it privately...." If they're only paying $200 a month, it's because their employer is paying the rest. The point is that the value remains the same. Make sure you think through these variables when you're presenting to a prospect.

REPEAT THE VALUE PROPOSITION ONE LAST TIME AS YOU PRESENT PRICE

This is incredibly important. Although you've mentioned the value several times in your price buildup, be prepared to state it one last time. When you're about to share your price with the prospects, summarize what you just shared with them and let them know that "Instead of paying X for all those great items or services, the price is only... Y!"

QUOTE THE HIGHEST PACKAGE PRICE YOU BELIEVE THE CLIENT NEEDS

In Chapter 9, we explored the idea of expanding your product offer at the end of the demonstration to expand your pricing options. My company offers several different packages that encourage this option. For example, clients not only can get varying levels of coverage on a cancer plan, but they can also tack on an accident or heart plan, or even buy life insurance coverage.

By simply explaining in a 30-second summary at the end of the demo that we have other plans that work and pay out like the cancer plan, we can present thepricing on the full package.

ALWAYS show the highest package price that you believe the client needs when you wrap up your price buildup.

This idea is important on several levels. The crucial phrase is, "...what you believe the client *needs*." Don't base your sales on lining your pockets by selling unneeded items. If you don't believe they need it, don't sell it. You might make some short-term cash, but lose in the long-term, because you'll lose business, you'll earn a bad reputation, and you won't last in your industry.

When you're confident about the products that your prospect needs, it might seem logical to start judging what you think they can afford and offering a less expensive and, therefore, less comprehensive plan. By instead quoting the highest priced package that you believe the client needs, you take this issue out of it.

I promise, it's natural to undersell prospects, but often, they'll be offended if they realize you prejudged their ability to buy. You believe you're doing the right thing; but you're making assumptions about what they can afford, and in some cases, limiting coverage that may be vital in the future.

While training a new agent years ago, we came upon a "house" that really was more like a mound of dirt with a front door. The father invited us in, and the three of us sat at their kitchen table with two of his kids. The kitchen had no windows and doubled as the living room. They were very nice, but obviously not well off.

Because I was training a new agent, I went through the entire demonstration, even though I probably would have politely left if I'd been by myself. I thought this would be a good way to teach her the process and how to respectfully leave a non-prospect.

We built a great rapport, and in the process of finding the need, we discovered how many members of his family had been ravished by cancer. We also learned how concerned he was about protecting his family from experiencing the same fate.

When we concluded the price buildup, he acknowledged that he didn't have a bank account, but asked if there were any other options. I reluctantly let him know that he could pay quarterly, but that would require taking care of three payments immediately, and then he'd be billed from that point forward. The dad then stepped away from the table, walked over to the refrigerator and brought down an old coffee can. Walking over to the table, he pulled out the cash he'd been saving, counted out the proper amount for the first quarterly payment, shook my hand, and thanked us for coming to see him.

By showing the highest package size, you have your full range of negotiating power to work with your prospects toward the package that makes the most sense for them. You'll be amazed how many of them will jump at your top package when you least expect it, but they can only do that if *you* give them the option.

BE INTUITIVE

State the price and gauge their reaction. If eyebrows fly up, they can't believe such a reasonable price quote. Go right into the close and sign them up!

Or, you may get that hesitant yet still positive look.

"That sounds pretty good, but I wasn't really looking to spend that kind of money today."

In this case, simply follow up with, "I mentioned earlier that we have several different packages based on your budget. Were you thinking about the entire package, or something smaller?"

If the answer is, "the entire package," then revisit the close and sign them up. If the answer is "something smaller," then start to create budget numbers by asking the yes or yes style questions. If the full package price was $500, you might ask,

"Were you looking for something more around the $400 range or somewhere more in the threes?"

This is important because you don't want to chop up the value of your product. You sell a great product or service, so *don't devalue it!* If the prospect answers, "Well, I was thinking something more in the $100 range," work from there, but don't immediately drop your price thinking that the issue lies there.

PROSPECTS LOVE A DEAL

Another reason to start with the highest package price is that most people like the feeling of getting a deal. My wife will be smiling ear to ear, excited about how much she saved on a pair of boots, delighted that they were 50% off. Regardless of how many times I ask the price, she'll quote the discount. Marketers know this, and that's why we all love Black Friday, Cyber Monday, or any major sale that Amazon promotes.

When you share your product's price, with some exceptions, the prospect will navigate to purchase a product that costs *less* than the full price you quoted. They'll either work with you to see if there's something you personally can do, or maybe ask:

"Is there a military discount?"
"What if I buy in bulk?"
"What if I pay in cash?"

Or they'll see if they can get the same product or service with fewer benefits.

"What if I get a smaller level of service?"

"What if I order online or direct?"

By initially offering the highest price, you have negotiating room, and it's much more palatable to negotiate down from $500 than down from $100. Let's take our alarm example:

If you go through the price buildup but only show the base home alarm offer for $100 a month (rather than the $500 package), the prospect will say yes, no, or negotiate down. That same process would exist if you had started with the $500 price. The major difference is that the first example at $100 leaves little to no room to negotiate. They either buy or they don't. At the $500 level, there's plenty of room to find a system that fits the prospect. Give yourself that room to work.

If you've already given your price buildup, it's very difficult to go back and *add* additional services. It's not impossible, but it's much easier at the front end rather than the tail end.

Going back to the $500 vs. $100 price buildup, consider this:

In the example, the prospect may negotiate to a level that gets a home alarm with no monitoring for $75 a month. They're feeling good because they were sold on a $100 value and got it for $75 (25% discount!). This is how your prospects think.

With the full package offered at $500, the prospect might respond that they were really thinking more along the lines of $200 to $250 max, at least to get started. You put together a package, and the prospect signs up for a plan right at $200. Again, the prospect feels good because they were sold on a $500 value and got it for $200 (a 60% discount!). Price wasn't the issue; the issue was value and feeling that they got a deal. Always show the highest package price.

TRANSITION TO THE CLOSE

With a set-price product (no packages or additional services), go through your price buildup, show its value, and state its price. At this point, you need a transitional statement to lead you into what we call the "assumptive close." I point that out in the price buildup section because the transitional statement must transition you to putting "pen to paper" without seeming awkward. In this case, I generally like to ask a completely *safe* question that doesn't put them on guard or make them feel uncomfortable.

> "Great! To get you started, George, I just need your address. Do you get your mail here or at the post office?"

This style of question is not intrusive, because, in most cases, I'm already in their home, so I know their address. They won't think twice about giving it to me.

You can ask the same type of question by simply confirming that their name is spelled the way that you would assume.

> "So, let me make sure I have this right. George is G E O R G E, just like it sounds, right?"

That may seem a little ridiculous, but it works. Again, the key here is to transition to the close.

Chapter 11

"A-B-C. A-Always, B-Be, C-Closing. Always be closing."

Blake, Glengarry Glen Ross

The Close

THE ASSUMPTIVE CLOSE

The transition from the price buildup to the assumptive close is crucial. It's not just *what* you say but *what you do* when you say it. Conceptually, the assumptive close assumes that you believe that the prospect is ready to buy. Don't ask for a yes or a no. Based on all their yes responses leading to this point, proceed with the next logical step in the process.

The assumptive close is my favorite because you get some butterflies in your stomach. It's exciting because, although you're writing up the order, you're not sure if you'll get stopped in the process.

As you delve into the paperwork, skip around to fill in the most generic information such as name, address, and phone, and leave the packages and pricing for last. This commits the prospect to the process. When you get to the packages and pricing section, assumptively write in the information that you know, based on what they agreed to (and speak the details out loud so they can correct or adjust based on what they hear you say).

If you haven't yet reached an agreement as to what they want, start guiding them through the yes or yes methodology.

"So, George, do you want to start with just Package A today, or would you like the Package A and B combo pack?"

Lead your prospect down this path to get them through the process as painlessly as possible.

Again, if you believe in what you're selling and if you've presented professionally and confidently, this close should be a breeze. The assumptive close, in my experience, is the most valuable closing technique in direct sales.

NOBODY LIKES TO MAKE A DECISION

If you love rock 'n' roll, you probably know the song *Freewill* by Rush. One of my favorite lines is, "If you choose not to decide, you still have made a choice." People tend to put off making decisions, and as we learned in the Buying Atmosphere chapter, the client's decision-making is a vital part of your success in direct sales. Your job is to get someone to a definite yes or no. Maybes don't fall into either of those categories, *but* that's what most clients want to give you.

The job of outside salespeople is to take the prospect by the hand and walk them through the sales cycle. We find/create the need, show them how we can fill it, shock them with our value proposition, and get their order fulfilled. The assumptive close is the greatest vehicle for this because it allows a smooth transition to the order-taking process.

BREAK EYE CONTACT AND PUT PEN TO PAPER

Look the prospect in the eye as you ask the transitional question. As you close your question, break eye contact, look at your order pad, put your pen in the correct spot, and *hold* until they answer. Sometimes it seems like an eternity, but once that answer comes, the rest of the form goes incredibly smoothly. This works whether you're using paper, a tablet, a laptop, whatever. The important thing is to ask and wait.

DON'T BE AFRAID OF SILENCE

This is true in any section of the cycle of sales. If you ask a question, let the client answer. Don't be in a rush to fill dead air. See what they have to say. This is especially true as you're closing. If the client wants to slow down the process, they won't need your help to do it. Silence and pausing are also valuable tools at any point of your visit. They help the listener process what's been said and mentally fill in the gaps of what they believe you're about to say. Bottom line is that it engages the listener.

ALTERNATIVE CLOSING METHODS

There are many ways to close, and I've used dozens of different styles over the years. The assumptive close is hands down the most effective method in direct sales. If you're interested in other methods, Zig Ziglar's *The Secrets of Closing the Sale*, which was one of my favorite reference books when I started, is a powerful reference of closing techniques. Here are other effective techniques.

THE CRYSTAL BALL

This takes some preliminary work, but once you've created your framework, it's one of the most fun closing techniques that I regularly layer into my presentations. In this close, you're asking the prospect to imagine two difference scenarios. One is what would happen if they went with your product or service, and, conversely, what would happen if they didn't. In either case, the obvious answer is that they should have what you're offering. Like looking through a crystal ball, we imagine weeks, months, or even years into the future, depending on what works best in your situation. Let's look at insurance:

> "Mrs. Jones, pretend that there's a crystal ball on the table and we can see five years into the future. Let's say that, unfortunately, someone in your family is fighting cancer. Because you had bought this plan, it is paying a substantial amount to your family to help with all the bills and additional costs. How do you think you'd feel knowing that you'd bought this product to protect your family?"

She'll likely state that she'd feel really good having made that decision.

"Now, let's change the scenario. Let's say that we look in that same crystal ball and again see five years into the future. In this case, everyone is perfectly healthy. The plan is still in place, and since you haven't used it, you have accumulated over $5K in your account, which you'd put away knowing that it would ultimately end up back in your pocket. How do you think you'd feel in that case knowing you'd put away all that savings and still had that protection in case something happened?"

Again, she'll likely state that she'd still feel great about having made the decision to get it.

"So really, Mrs. Jones, the only way you wouldn't feel great is if you didn't have it at all."

Honestly, this close is even fun to write. It's so powerful that you should try to incorporate it with nearly any product. For example:

Politician—What she could do for you if she wins. / What might happen if her opponent wins.
Alarms—What if your home were invaded? / The feeling of security that you feel in your own home.
Cable Service—The entertainment that's available to your family. / Reliability of being connected even in the worst weather.

BEN FRANKLIN CLOSE

This is one of the oldest closes, and one of the strongest. It relies on helping the prospect determine if it makes sense to move forward by looking at a simple pros and cons list. On a sheet of paper, draw a line down the middle. At the top of the left column, create a list for pros and on the right, for cons.

Pro	Con
1	1
2	2
3	3
4	4
5	5
6	6

Ask what the positives would be if they picked up your product or service. By the way, I recommend sitting next to them during the process, on the same side of the table, and doing this together.

Let them start to list the items on their own. Be supportive and help them where necessary with suggestions that they can add to the list. When they're done (and don't stop them until they're finished), say, "Great! Now let's list the reasons why this wouldn't be a good idea." Let them list their items, *but* without your help. Remain supportive, but just shut up and let them list. If your product is good for them and you did a good job demonstrating, their pros list should be exponentially longer than their cons list.

In most cases, when you wrap this up, they'll intuitively know that it's in their best interest is to move forward with the plan.

NEXT STEPS

In nearly every close, you will transition back to the assumptive close anyway, so become expert at it. When most closes are used, you're going to finish with a closing yes question:

"George, can you see why everyone's been getting this from me?"
"Can you see why the Bakers picked this up?"
"Isn't that great?"

In all these cases, your mind should be translating their "Yes" into, "Yes, I'm ready to buy now." That will allow you to use the same transitional question, "Great! To get you started, I just need your address. Do you get your mail here or at the post office?"

Closing is a ton of fun, so have fun with it!

Chapter 12

"The difference between the impossible and the possible lies in a person's determination"

Tommy Lasorda

Rebuttals

Your first question should be, "What? Rebuttals? That's not part of the sales cycle," and you'd be right to question why this is a chapter and not a subsection. The simple answer is that dealing with rebuttals is as important as any other piece of the sales cycle, and you will need to handle rebuttals at different times throughout the sales cycle. Among other terms, this can also be called, **answering objections.**

What is a rebuttal?
When a prospect stops your process, sensing that you're going down a path for which they're not ready, you're about to encounter a rebuttal. Determine if this is a legitimate rebuttal or if the prospect simply isn't interested in your product. If they're not interested or it's later in the presentation and they're saying that they just don't need what you're selling, then get some referrals, pack up, and move on. If it's a legitimate rebuttal, it will generally fall into two categories: price and procrastination.

Price Rebuttal

A prospect that pushes back because of price might have a variety of reasons such as they:

a) Can't afford it
b) Don't see the value in the product
c) Don't have the money in the bank to purchase
d) Don't have a bank account

Procrastination Rebuttal

The prospect wants to put off deciding. These are more common than price rebuttals, with some classic responses:

a) "I never make a decision without speaking to my spouse."
b) "I have to pray on this."
c) "I don't make snap decisions without taking a few days to think about a purchase."

The price objections could very well be true. It's your job to provide good options to help them out such as available financing, holding the application for a few weeks until they hit pay day, or offering a reduced cost plan to get them started. Be ready to share options.

Procrastination rebuttals are garbage. It's human nature to want to put off a decision, but unless you're selling a multimillion-dollar item, which is rare in direct sales, then understand that a procrastination objection is something you should *welcome* because it's easily overcome.

Now, you might be thinking, "Dan, why can't I let them think about it?" "Isn't it bad to try to push them to a decision when all they want to do is talk to their spouse?"

Let's recap what's happened up to this point in the sales cycle. The most important thing when it comes to these objections is that you established a buying atmosphere early on. The prospect told you that they could decide. It's that simple. Something else to understand is that people who say they don't make snap decisions, do so all the time. Sixty percent of groceries are purchased because they're seen at the store; not planned to be picked up. We all grab the convenience items now and then that are at the checkout line. Most spouses don't call their significant others to ask if it's okay to fill the gas tank, grab something for the home, and so on.

You might argue that your product or service requires this extra time, but I'll counter that if there's even one sales rep in your company that regularly does a same-day close, then you need to take this last paragraph to heart.

Nothing will more quickly destroy a direct sales salesperson, than their willingness to be "sold" on following up later.

There's always a sale occurring when you're with a prospect. In this case, it's *them* selling *you*.

So how do we handle these objections or rebuttals? We use a very simple four-step process: Acknowledge, Educate, Re-Engage, Re-Close.

Step 1: Acknowledge the Objection

When a prospect objects, make sure that they feel "heard" by you. Avoid a tug-of-war with the client that puts you in an adversarial position. For example, if they give you a procrastination objection, don't say, "But, Bob, remember earlier when you promised you'd just give me that yes or no today? Well, you're not really doing that."

That's an effective way to get that no you were promised! This paints the prospect into a corner, feeling the need to fight their way out, and can become somewhat adversarial. Instead, acknowledge their objection and get on the proverbial same side of the table with them.

> "Bob, I know how you feel. My wife and I always like to go over things together whenever we make a major decision, so we're on the same page."

It takes *one* to agree.

This touches on a key concept: the power of agreement. Most arguments with your significant other, teachers, friends, whoever, generally start because you have opposing viewpoints on an issue. We tend to graduate directly into this tug-of-war scenario. Remember, it only takes one person (not two) to end an argument in its tracks. Think about it. You feel one way, and I feel another. All I must do is change my feeling or view, and now we're in agreement.

When you're dealing with an objection, agree with it, and then work from there. It sets you up as leading them toward the finish line as opposed to pushing them.

Step 2: Educate—Give the Prospect New Information to Make a New Decision

This is a powerful step, one that I wish we'd been smarter about when we were kids. I see it today with my teen whenever she asks me for something:

"Dad, can I go to Lauren's?" she'll ask.

"Jenica, it's a Wednesday night, and you have school tomorrow. Let's talk about it over the weekend," I'll reply.

"WHY CAN'T I GO?! That's so DUMB!" would be her normal go-to response. "WHY?!"

You get the point. The more she berates me, the more aggravated I get, and is she getting any closer to going to Lauren's? Heck no! She's probably blowing her chance of doing anything with Lauren over the weekend as well.

Now, let's say that instead of her original follow-up line, things went this way:

"Dad, may I go to Lauren's?"

"Jenica, it's a Wednesday night and you have school tomorrow. Wait until the weekend," is still my reply.

"Well, I'm asking because we have a project due tomorrow, and my group, Lauren, Alina, and I, are supposed to meet at seven o'clock to finish it. Mom already said it was okay; I just needed to get a ride, please?"

What is my answer most likely going to be now? That's a *ton* of new information that's allowed me to make a new decision without feeling like my pride was injured or that I'd need to hold my ground. When you work with your prospects, allow them the same courtesy. Most of them will feel that when they serve you an objection, your return volley will be harsh. Work with them to present an alternative based on information they didn't originally have.

Remember how Bob wanted to chat first with his wife, and we acknowledged that we felt the same way? Now we give him some new information.

"One thing that I didn't mention earlier, Bob, is since we're just taking the application today, it simply allows us to start the qualification process. I'll leave a welcome packet for you and your wife to review. I don't submit these applications until next Monday, so you have plenty of time. If for some reason, she thinks you made a horrible decision, just call me and I'll tear up the application. That's a lot easier than trying to track you down later this week just to fill it out, right?"

Note: After saying "right" at the end of that sentence, don't invite or wait for a reply. Just go on to the next step.

Step 3: Re-Engage—Return to Your Product and Provide a New Buying Atmosphere

At this point in the cycle of sales, you are far removed from your product or service and must re-engage and re-excite your prospect to close the deal. Take them back and present another great benefit that you withheld the first time around, what I referred to earlier as "keeping bullets in your gun." If you reveal every benefit during your initial demonstration, there's nothing left to show to counter an objection at the end. Retain several of your favorite benefits to share at this point so you have a stronger opportunity to close the sale.

Equally important is letting the prospect know *what* to expect next. Remember, you are taking the client on a journey, a journey that you take with them "hand in hand." Let them know what will happen if they love your benefit, and what will happen if they don't. That way, when you go to Step 4, they'll already know what's going to happen next.

We just gave Bob new information to put him at ease doing your paperwork. Now we need to rebuild his interest to show him it's worth taking that step.

"So, Bob, let me do this: I'll show you another product benefit. It's part of the same package we're talking about, and I think it's one of the greatest benefits. After you see it, if you're still on the fence, I'll take that as a 'no' and not move forward with the application. Frankly, if you don't love it, your wife isn't going to either. On the other hand, if you look at that benefit and think, 'Wow. That's a no-brainer,' then we'll go ahead and fill out the application information like we discussed, and I'll leave the welcome packet for you and your wife. Fair enough?"

Again, even though I end with a question, I break eye contact and go right into showing the new benefit. Bob now knows what the plan is, and we're only going to move forward if he loves what I show him (and that *equals* filling out the application).

Step 4: Ask a Closing Question and Reclose

This is the simplest step, but important to understand. After I've demonstrated the new benefit and gotten Bob excited, I'll ask him a simple yes question to make sure he's on board with me:

"Bob, can you see why everyone has been getting this from me?!"

Notice the "!" at the end. That's there for a reason. Ask your closing question with excitement to try and illicit that same excitement from your prospect.

When Bob says, "Yes," what I'm hearing is, "Yes, I'm ready to fill out the paperwork," so I simply follow up by reclosing:

"Great! So, to get you started, I just need your address. Do you get your mail here or at the post office?"

I then break eye-contact and wait for him to speak.

Now, does this always lead to the sale? No, not always, but most of the time it does. I've sometimes had to repeat this four-step process two or more times to get them to close. By staying pleasantly persistent and starting to close early when they're over the buying line, you'll have time to try this several times, and gain a new client.

A little side note about rebuttals and using this system. All these methods are effective if used responsibly and ethically. Use this system in all walks of life to encourage others to see your viewpoint—and definitely in the course of selling.

During reclosing, you can also use the Feel/Felt/Found" (FFF) method, which is more effective for "filler rebuttals," those little objections that may occur along the way:

Bob assures me, "I never buy anything door to door."

"Bob, I know how you *feel*," I empathize. "As a matter of fact, Scott and Susan across the street *felt* the exact same way until they *found* that our company has been around for over 100 years and that we're the leading provider of X in Travis County."

Returning to the application or invoice, fill out as much as you can, leaving the cash collection for last. This is the next hurdle to overcome, so get the client as committed as possible by filling everything else out first. Again, don't assume you'll have an issue here, but be prepared if it comes up.

Chapter 13

"People are always blaming their circumstances for being what they are. The people who get on in this world are the people who get up and look for the circumstances they want, and if they can't find them, make them"

George Bernard Shaw

Collecting Cash

Closing doesn't just occur in the process of getting the prospect to agree to purchase, it occurs several times after that as well. Probably the two main points of interest are in the next chapter on gathering referrals and this Collecting Cash chapter.

To effectively get paid by the prospect, be aware of all your options. For example, what do you do if the prospect:

- Doesn't use credit cards?
- Doesn't have a bank account?
- Doesn't use a checkbook?
- Doesn't know their account information.
- Won't have enough money in their account until the 15th.

This list can go on and on. Understand first what your options are and provide the prospect an easy way to overcome any objection. You shouldn't (in most cases) have to use our four-step rebuttal system, and if you do, they frankly weren't sold on your product. *Patiently and confidently* ask some questions that will lead you to getting the needed payment to execute the next stage of the sale.

"Does your company allow you to take cash? How do you handle cash? (Do you buy a money order or deposit the cash directly?)"

If you collect account information and they don't have checks on hand, consider these options:

"Do you have 'back-up' checkbooks in the house or office? Most people buy checks in bulk and these may be nearby, even if your day-to-day checkbook is not."
"Do you have a bank statement available?"
"Do you do online banking, and can you pull up a statement there?"

Is the bank nearby? (This sounds crazy, but I've driven a prospect *to the bank* to get their account information. Your job is to close the sale; not to pray that they call later with the information. That's a fool's errand.

Can you take annual, semiannual, or quarterly payments? Does your company offer payment plans? Can they pay in installments? Is there a discount for a year's payment made in full? Do we accept collateral? Can they sign over their car title?! I'm reaching here, but the bottom line is that you need to know your options so you can be "pleasantly persistent" and get the payment you need to move forward.

Business-to-Business (B2B) Cash Collection

In the case of business enrollments or deals, I like to coordinate payment information ahead of time. In the insurance industry, this can be easily handled by doing an enrollment through the company payroll. I avoid going through payroll if I can help it because people don't traditionally stay with the same company as they did a few generations ago. Today, an employee might stay with the same company for six to twelve years before moving on to greener pastures. If I sign up someone through payroll, when they leave,

I'll generally lose that client. If I write them up directly, however, they're personally connected to the account. This benefits *me* in keeping a longer-term client, but it also benefits the *client*, because when they leave, they're not in jeopardy of having a break or a loss in their coverage, because it's not tied to their paycheck. That's the definition of a win-win!

Trust and Rapport

If you sense that your prospect is uncomfortable sharing account information, you've probably encountered a trust problem. In most cases, it's not that they have an issue providing their account information; the problem is that they have an issue giving it to *you*.

Obviously, the rapport you established wasn't as solid as you thought. Not all is lost. Find a way to get your client back on your side. Going back into the four-step rebuttal system is one way to overcome the pull-back.

Acknowledge that many people have concerns nowadays giving out secure information. Get on their side of the table.

Give them new information to make that new decision. Brag about what makes your company great and tie it to other clients. Share testimonials. Use your FFF method to point out that their neighbor Rachel felt the same way until she found out that most of the top ranking officers in the local police department were also signed up on the programs and had used their accounts to sign up.

If necessary, go back briefly into the product, but you won't have to if you do a good job in your FFF overview.

Chapter 14

"Best friends are the siblings that God forgot to give us"

Mencius (Chinese Philosopher)

Referrals

The backbone of any successful business, especially when it comes to direct sales, lies in your ability to gather qualified referrals to lead you toward your next sale. Unless you want to spend your life cold calling and building "from scratch," you must become a Ph.D. at getting referrals and learning how to follow up with them.

Cold Calling: Is it Necessary?
I hate to break it to you, but cold calling is essential if you're planning a successful career in direct sales. There's no way around that. Even if you work with a company that supplies leads or you're working over someone else's "book" (their list of previously serviced clients), to achieve maximum efficiency, you must do some cold calling.

Here's the good news. Cold calling should not be something you focus on or do very long, but it's necessary in certain situations, so let's look at the number one reason why.

YOU HAVE NO LEADS—This is the most common reason for getting out there and cold calling. Don't waste time trying to figure out how to find leads; simply go out and knock, dial, or do whatever you can to create business. You may have no leads because you're brand new in the business. Perhaps you had a bunch of appointments cancel, and you don't have anything set up. You drove out to see a client that stood you up. Create some lemonade from this sour circumstance. Cold call to keep your numbers up and work to get in front of as many potential clients as possible.

This is the harsh truth of what we do. Cold calling isn't fun for most of us, but it *will* keep you sharp, and people will buy. Understand this though: Whenever you make a presentation to a cold call or *anyone*, you need to get **referrals!** A few cold call presentations should get you enough referrals to reduce your cold calling time to almost nothing.

Laying the Groundwork for Referrals

Earlier, we learned about the introduction (establishing rapport) and how that helps set up your referrals. The introduction is where you can take advantage of that. A common response when a salesperson asks for referrals at the *end* of a sale is, "I don't really know anyone," or "We kind of keep to ourselves," or "We can't think of anyone who'd need that."

If you asked the proper questions in the introduction, you probably collected a good number of names from them. Remember some of those questions?

"Are you folks originally from here?"
"Does your family live in the area as well?"
"Where do you work? What do you do there?"
"Are you folks active with your kids' school? How long have you been in the PTA/PTO?"
"You seem very active with the church? How big is the congregation?"

By asking these questions and prompting your client to elaborate, you should get referrals easily as you wrap up.

Telling for Referrals

A common practice is to ask for referrals when you wrap up a sales call. I use a method that I coined "Telling for Referrals," where you assumptively start a referral list by referring to their personal network that you learned about in the Introduction. The prospect understands what you're doing from the get-go, but you're taking the pressure off and making the process easy. Keep these important factors in mind during this process:

1) Be assumptive. The procurement of referrals is a sale, just as much as getting in the door and having a client agree to purchase your product or service, so treat it the same way. be confident as you're collecting names; be assumptive, break eye contact, put your pen to paper, and start filling out your referral sheet.

2) Have a system. Don't start jotting names on the back of a sheet of paper or into a random section of your iPad or tablet. Have a tracking system to easily retrieve the information that you need. I use a "Tic-Tac-Toe" referral system when I collect that I'll explain in a bit.

3) Focus on names rather than details. When getting referrals, time is limited before the prospect tires, so get as many names as you can. Go back later and fill in the details: address, phone number, employer, marital status, children, and so on. Once you have the names, the other information comes easily.

4) Focus on addresses. Remember, an address is ten times better than a phone number, although both are useful. Think about a close friend. If you call to get together, even casually, they'll often put you off. It's human nature.

5) "Right now's not great; call me in a few hours."

6) "I'm slammed on Tuesday, but let's try and get together at the end of the week."

7) We don't take this personally because it's normal, but when a prospect does it, we assume they have a problem with us. Remember, this is

just what people *do*. With an address, it's different. Take that same friend and just stop by. Generally, they'll invite you in, you'll sit down, and it's amazing that they have time. That's the power of an address.

8) Make the process fun, and, hopefully, rewarding. People love games, they love to have fun, and they love a prize (i.e. gift cards, something for their kids, dinner for two). When you reward your clients for helping you, you'll get a lot more out of them. Be sure to follow state and local laws, depending on what you're selling. Consider how valuable a good lead is to you and don't be cheap when it comes to getting doors opened for you.

Tic-Tac-Toe Referral Gathering

I can't take credit for coming up with this idea, but it's one I've used for years for several kinds of products and services. It works! I have a referral sheet that has a referral "box" set up in the layout of a tic-tac-toe board. I let the client know that when I collect referrals from them, if the referrals match up for a tic-tac-toe, they win a gift card. Even better, if they win multiple times, they win multiple gift cards. Tic-tac-toe allows a client to win up to eight times per referral sheet.

TIC TAC TOE REFERRALS
(for every tic tac toe line of referrals who sign up, you win a $25 gift certificate to the restaurant of your choice)

Referred by: _____

Name _____	Name _____	Name _____
Relationship _____	Relationship _____	Relationship _____
Address _____	Address _____	Address _____
Phone _____ Age __	Phone _____ Age __	Phone _____ Age __
Work _____	Work _____	Work _____
Name _____	Name _____	Name _____
Relationship _____	Relationship _____	Relationship _____
Address _____	Address _____	Address _____
Phone _____ Age __	Phone _____ Age __	Phone _____ Age __
Work _____	Work _____	Work _____
Name _____	Name _____	Name _____
Relationship _____	Relationship _____	Relationship _____
Address _____	Address _____	Address _____
Phone _____ Age __	Phone _____ Age __	Phone _____ Age __
Work _____	Work _____	Work _____

Here are the steps for setting up great referrals:

Step 1: Remind the Prospect Why They Liked the Product or Service
Notice that the step doesn't say, "Why they *bought*," because buying has nothing to do with it. You will get amazing referrals from people who never purchased your product, so make sure to go through this step with everyone you make a presentation to. The only exception? The prospect just doesn't like what you're selling. In that case, move on.

Remind them by asking a yes or yes question:

"Winslow, let me ask, what do you like more about the product, the fact that it has the included service contract or the fact that it's guaranteed for life?" A prospect doesn't need to buy to have an appreciation and understanding of why your product is beneficial.

Step 2: Explain How You Do Business
This is where personality helps. Remain professional, while still being lighthearted and fun.

> "Susan, I have to tell you, everyone has been great out here, and most of the clients I've seen are from referrals they've given me. I love giving back, so I devised this game. Check it out!"

I pull out my referral sheet.

> "See, it's basically a giant tic-tac-toe board. When I get referrals, I put them on this sheet, and whenever tic-tac-toe comes up, I give my clients a $25 gift card for wherever they want. There are actually eight ways to win, so you can win up to $200 per sheet."

Step 3: Put Pen to Paper
> "Susan, if you and Scott were to win, what kind of gift card would you want, just a VISA gift card for cash or maybe something more specific like for Chili's or Amazon?"

> "Actually," she says, "we love going to Cheddar's Restaurant."

> "Great!" I reply and immediately write "Cheddar's gift card" in the corner of the page and her and her husband's name after "Referred by."

The power of these initial three steps is that it allows you to comfortably transition to and get out the referral sheet and begin filling it out without feeling awkward. Now you finally get to collect!

Step 4: Getting Referrals
Now is when you "tell" them the people you're going to call on:

> "Susan, you'd mentioned your brother Brian. Does he live on this side of town or on the south side?"

> "Brian actually lives just a couple of streets away," she answers.

> "Okay," I say as I'm jotting down his name and their relationship (brother), "and what's his last name? I assume it's different than yours?" Note that information as well.

"And, you'd mentioned your mom and dad live out here. What are their first names?"

This process continues from block to block, as Susan works on getting the sheet filled out. As she pauses through the process, I continue to remind her of names.

"You'd said that you're managing now at your company. Who are some of the folks that you manage that you're closest to?"

"You'd mentioned that you're at First Cavalry Church over on Main. What's the pastor's name?"

As I referenced earlier, focus on writing down basic information at this point such as names and their relationship to the referrer. The goal is to get as many names as you can. Don't tire out! And, keep multiple referral sheets because some of your prospects will fill sheet after sheet after sheet.

NOTE: *If you're with a client that's giving you lots of good referrals, don't get trapped into thinking that you've been with the client too long. If your average time with a client is 45 minutes, and you're spending an additional hour or more with them getting referrals, that's fine. Referrals are your lifeblood, so get as many quality referrals as possible!*

Now ASK.

After you've exhausted the work you did in your introduction, use memory joggers to help them recall more names:

"Who else in your family lives in the area?"

"What about your spouse's family? Where do they live?"

- PTA/PTO
- Parents of your kids' friends
- Teachers at the school
- Co-workers
- Co-workers from their last job

- Friends from church
- People in their networking groups (BNI, Kiwanis, Elks Club, etc.)
- Clubs they are affiliated with (motorcycle, quilting, scrapbooking, etc.)
- Most frequently called people in their phones
- Top friends on Facebook, Instagram, or other social media
- Neighbors
- Sports teammates
- Barber or Hairdresser
- Manicurist
- Their dry cleaner
- Handywoman/man

The list goes on and on. These suggestions can often open doors leading to many more names, just when they thought they'd completely exhausted their list.

The Power of Games

The tic-tac-toe format also enables you to push for more names to increase their chances to win. Let's say your client gives you only four names. Filling in one more box gives them an additional chance to win. The same holds true with a fifth box. Again, it is psychological. People love to win, so help them work toward that.

When you've completely exhausted your names, go back and fill in the rest of the referral sheet. If there's information you know you won't use, don't waste time asking for it. Basically, if you don't need their shoe size, why ask? Get the information you need and be patient. Have them keep their phone handy, as that will probably contain phone number and address information for most clients. Again, focus primarily on addresses as you'll get in front of more prospects if you simply drive there. Ask when the best time is to catch the referral. You don't want to drive around trying to find them if you can simply get that information at this point. It's best to stop by when both decision makers will be home, so add that information as well.

Chapter 14

Gathering Referrals Early

If you've offered a free service or gift to your prospect in order to get your appointment, then gather referrals immediately so that they can pass on that same gift to the people that they care about! Do this before showing the product or service that you're there to sell and allow yourself the opportunity to schedule several more appointments.

Now, you may find this to be very early in your overall presentation, and that's okay. Your focus at this point has been on value, and your prospect should be on the same page. Take that positive momentum and use the tools that you've learned to build your referral base.

Continue to be assumptive in your referral gathering, and mention some of the people that you've learned about through your time with them and that you'll get them the same gift. Simply ask for the additional details that you need, get their contact information, and continue to get more and more names until your prospect runs out. This is one of a couple times that you'll be getting referrals in your presentation.

Instant Client Follow Up

Have your prospect help you get into your next appointment by making introduction for you. After you finish gathering your referrals, send them a pre-written text that they can send to the people that they referred to let them know you'll be calling. In this beautiful digital age we live in, I've got a ton of shortcuts programmed into my phone / computer to make this process even quicker. Jump forward to the end of this chapter for a quick overview of how to do this.

Text the wording to your prospect, and ask them to forward it to each of the numbers that they gave you. Be patient and work through the list with them. As they're doing this, reassure them that they'll probably get some confused texts back from their referrals, and just laugh it off. Let them know you'll follow up shortly to see if what you have is a good fit.

Phone Introductions

If you're wrapping up your presentation and don't have something scheduled for immediately after, you can also use this same type of process to set an immediate appointment:

"Mark, is there anyone on your list that should be available right now?"

Mark replies, "Actually, my sister has the day off today, so she should be home."

"Great!" you answer. "Let me introduce myself while I have you on Zoom (or whatever web client you're using)."

Call his sister, Mary…

"Hi Mary?"

"Yes, who is this?"

"Hi Mary, this is Dan calling, I'm actually here with Mark - MARK, say Hi!"

"Hey, sis," Mark yells through the computer speaker.

"Mark said he'd texted you a little bit ago, did you get that text?"

"Yes, I received it,"

"Great! I was just wrapping up with Mark and he was saying this was a pretty good time to catch you as you had the day off today. Mark, I'll let you go and let Mark know what we went over, give me a call if you need anything."

Disconnect with Mark, and turn your attention to your new appointment:

"So, Mary…"

Mapping

So much is happening virtually, but if your business still requires you to be face to face or sitting across the kitchen table, getting addresses can be tough. Much like phone numbers, most folks don't memorize addresses. If you're struggling to get an address with the name, the Internet can provide some options to overcome this:

WhitePages.com— This is an amazing time-saving reference if you've done your homework. Enter your referral's name, and it'll list everyone by that name in your city. A segment of the search function lets you match with other names that reside in the same house. In other words, if you know the spouse's name, you can often pinpoint the correct address.

Google or Yahoo Maps—These are both useful because you'll often hear, "I don't know their address, but I know how to get there." Other similar services are available.

"Great! I'll open my tablet, zoom in on their house, and let's "drive" over to the referral's house together," tracing the streets on the map.

Because most mapping has a satellite view, you can also see all the houses on the street.

"YES! That's the house with the circular driveway and the pool in the back! It's the only house on the street with both of those features."

With these two mapping services, simply note on the referral sheet that, "Their house is the third on the right, west of the Duval and 1st Street intersection."

Spotio—This is one of the better pre-approach mapping services. Spotio shows you every house and building in their non-satellite view (no issue with trees), *and* if you click on any of those buildings or houses, the system automatically pulls up their street address. Great system for uploading all your contacts, and incredibly easy to access your information, especially when you're in the field.

Setting Shortcuts On Your Phone/Computer
Earlier, I'd referenced these shortcuts. In general, most devices will give you the ability to take a good amount of text and save it as a short key phrase. Depending on the type of device you use, you want to generally go into the settings of your device and SEARCH for something along the lines of, "Text Replacement." When you choose this, you should be able to systematize the items that you find yourself sending out over and over again. Let me give you some example of how I use this:

- I have a link I use when people need to set an appointment with me (I use the service, Calendly which I highly recommend). My shortcut I use is:

Calendar1

Whenever I typle "Calendar1" into my phone, it substitutes that phrase with the link I need to send. No more hunting for the link and then copy and pasting!

- Introductory text messages

Intro1

I'll use it here, and once the full text pops up, I'll fill in the prospects name at the beginning of the text

Here are a few others:

- Follow Up Messages (I can do several of these: FollowUp1, FollowUp2, etc)
- WebConference Address (Zoom1)
- Confirmation Appointment Text (Appointment1)
- Reschedule Text (Reschedule1)

You'll notice that I put a number at the end of my key phrase (i.e. "Calendar1"). The reason for this is because I don't want the system to replace the word, "calendar," that I might be using in a normal sentence (not as a key phrase). The second reason is that I may have several different texts that I want to send that may go in a specific order, just like the "Follow Up Message" I gave you in the list earlier. My first follow up may be immediately after our call. The second might be a few days later, and I'd label that, "FollowUp2."

This is a highly underutilized skill that most devices can do, that you might not be using. Use it!

Chapter 15

"Well, it's no trick to make a lot of money...
if all you want to do is make a lot of money"

Bernstein, Citizen Kane

Reservicing

Have you ever bought something from a salesperson, and once that sale was over, you never heard from them again? It happens *much* too often. I'm most aware of it on a small scale when I go out for dinner.

We all know the situation. You have an amazing dinner with friends, you're finishing up dessert, and then the server comes with your bill, especially smiley and nice because, what are you about to do? TIP! Servers always try to leave their best impression just as you're deciding how much to leave. My family isn't always finished when the bill arrives, generally in the middle of our meal. I'm Armenian, and we like to sit around and chat and spend some extra time together. How many of you have been in this same situation, where you almost have to *beg* anyone to come by and refill your drink? Your own server who just minutes before was draped all over you is now nowhere to be seen. Why? Because we're all taught that once the bill is paid, the deal is done. That is not the case. Your attitude should always be that once you close a deal, that's just the beginning of the relationship, not the end.

Think about a salesperson that works in the opposite manner? Maybe you purchased a car, and the salesperson checked in with you a few weeks later to see how your friends have enjoyed your new car? Perhaps they sent a reminder for your first major service or oil change. Who will you most likely call when it's time to get a new car for one of your kids or when your friend's looking to make a purchase? The answer is as obvious as why we need to build these relationships. This is what we refer to as "reservicing."

Reservicing is the nurturing of a relationship with your clients.

Thank You Cards

Thank you cards are the simplest, easiest, and most inexpensive form of follow-up when you get a new client. Regardless of the size of your sale, this gesture is always appreciated. It's a personal touch. Here are some suggestions that I have incorporated over the years.

1) Handwrite, or at least *appear* to handwrite, your notes. Don't send a card that only includes the preprinted cute saying and your signature. This indicates that you have a big stack just stamped and waiting to be sent, and it's almost as bad as sending nothing at all.

2) Include a personal note. Ninety percent of your notes can read the same but include something that you learned about your client while you were together. Send good wishes on their daughter going off to college. Relate the fun you had playing with their dog. Make it personal and specific, and not necessarily work related.

3) Include a personal picture on the card. Many companies will send photo cards for you. Putting a personal picture on the front of the card goes a long way in keeping you in the forefront of your clients' minds. I've sent these cards out for years, and in many cases, this has tied my clients to not just me, but to my family, as they've watched my kids grow over the years. If you're uncomfortable sending pictures of your kids, just send a picture of you and your spouse, or you and your pet(s), or even you in a funny situation.

4) Make your pictures memorable. Even if it's just a thank you card, try not to make it boring and ordinary. Over the years, I've included pictures of my family choking each other in front of the fireplace for Christmas (we're all laughing), pictures of us on vacation in front of some outlandish scenery, or a bunch of different funny pictures of the kids and me in different situations. One of my favorites was a selfie of me in the car with my daughter passed out in the backseat in her child seat. She had her head all the way back and her mouth wide open (the "catching flies" pose). I can't tell you the joy it gives me to go into a client's home or office and see one of my cards up on the fridge, on their desk, or in a place with their relatives and friends.

5) Always include your phone number. *Don't include your business card.* It doesn't have the same effect. As a matter of fact, I sometimes mention in the greeting card that the number I'm sending them is my personal cell phone number, just to personalize our experience a little more. Business cards are a waste of time in a direct sale situation. People who ask for them use that to put you off. Enclosed in a card, they'll probably get tossed, because if you decide to keep the card, what are you going to do with that loose card that's floating around? It's like the confetti in envelopes; litter that needs to be cleaned up.

Semi-Annual Follow-Up Cards

Hand in hand with thank you cards are semi-annual follow-up cards. You might think every six months is too often in your business, but in my experience, it's the perfect follow-up time. It's beneficial for you because twice a year it puts you in front of your client and on their radar. If I pop in to see a client, I know they've heard from me one way or another within the past six months. If I go and ask for referrals, try and sell them new items, or simply catch up, it's not at all awkward, whereas some of my contemporaries might feel strange. Their customers may feel as though, "Chuck only comes to see me when he needs something." You never want your clients to feel that way.

1) Send your cards in November and May. Why? Well first, I send cards in November because it's the first holiday card that they'll get, and it's not offensive in any way. Another useful tip I learned from Tom Hopkins was that Thanksgiving Day cards are happily received by everyone because *everyone* celebrates Thanksgiving. This isn't true with Christmas, Chanukah, or some other holidays, so you avoid offending anyone. Also, your card comes before all the other holiday cards that are sent in December. You stand out! I send my second card in May because it's six months after November. Simple math.

2) Make your semi-annual cards more personal regarding you and your life. The thank you card includes a simple reference to something about *them*, but your semi-annual card should be closer to what you might send your own family. I like to give a recap of what's happening with my family, a reference to the fact that I hope their family is doing well, and I include my phone number so they can contact me if they need anything. Without question, I'll get calls in November and in May from clients that need information on something, or even clients that have been considering canceling. I can't tell you how many sales I've saved because they called me and inquired about something that I easily answered. Since I get paid residually for sales I've made, just getting the opportunity to answer these questions has made these cards worth it a thousand times over.

How to Call on a Reserviced Client

In most cases, I don't phone to set up appointments to see past clients, I just drop in. I've found that setting appointments often leads to pushing things out days or weeks, whereas if I just drop by, people will, often, make time for me. When you see an old friend from school, maybe someone you haven't seen in years, you stop and reminisce, catch up and laugh, and promise to see each other soon, but how often does that happen? Even if you try to set it up right there on the spot, things seldom get scheduled right away.

"Lori, we have to get together; it's been so long!"

"No kidding! We should grab lunch. Are you around next week?"

"Next week I'm slammed, and, actually, I'll be gone the week after that as well. How about after the 1st? Better yet, just drop me an email, and we'll get something on the calendar for February."

This is all done with the best of intentions, but the reality is that this is how most of those conversations go. Forget about these interactions and *just show up*. If you get put off, simply ask, "Since I'm going to be in the area, is it better to catch you later tonight or maybe first thing tomorrow?" Go back to giving them two yes choices and make a solid appointment for as soon as possible. In a territory where you haven't worked in a while, proceed in a circular fashion to try to find clients at home. If you miss them in the morning, try again in the early afternoon and then again in the evening. By working tight in this fashion, you'll see a good percentage of those reservice clients in a short time.

How to Run a Reservice Appointment

Now that you've reconnected with a client, what next? First, let me say this:

Nothing is more powerful than reservicing your client base. Reservicing grows your business in the most substantial way and is the easiest part of direct selling.

In my industry, I go back to see a new client after 30 days. For you, this may be too late or even too early, but in insurance, it works out perfectly. Within that period, they've seen their first premium, they've received their policies in the mail, and they've read my thank you card. It's the ideal time to check back with them and review what they've purchased.

So many of my clients say that they very rarely see their agents when it comes to almost anything they've bought, be it insurance for their home, auto, or life; an alarm system; knives; solar; whatever. I've heard comments for years about how weird it is to be paying for something month after month and never hearing from the company that they're paying. Good salespeople give clients a different experience; not just because it's good for us (and it is!), but also because it's the *right* thing to do. In an era when people are getting inundated by email campaigns, robo-calls, and piles of junk mail, remember that nothing is more powerful than a personal touch.

My process when visiting a client is generally as follows:

1) Reconnect
2) Resell
3) Acknowledge the elephant in the room
4) Offer new options
5) Get new referrals

Reconnect

This basically re-establishes rapport and cements your friendship with your client. Direct sales becomes *enjoyable and rewarding;* therefore, learn to love this aspect of our business. Our connection with others is quite possibly the most important thing that we do during our lives. When your clients start sending you gifts and cards, begin to have their friends call you so they can also become clients, and share the good and the bad that's happening within their families, you know that you've created a special relationship.

Reconnect with clients differently than you did when you first met. It doesn't take much time. How have their lives changed since you last saw them? Can your products tie into what you're hearing? Because of what I sell, I'm listening for medical issues since I last spoke to them. Have they needed my products? Should they get something new now?

Resell

Here, you get your clients excited about the product that they've already purchased from you. Because of the nature of our business, I may have signed up someone for our services, but I didn't get a chance to sit with their spouse. Now's a great opportunity to show their significant other what they now have for their family. It may also be as simple as just getting my client re-excited about the product they purchased. Remember that the best way to build *any* business is *not* to lose the business that you've already built! If you get nothing more out of your reservice than getting someone more comfortable with their purchase, then you've already paid for your time.

When reselling, I'm not going through as much of the *need*; I'm primarily focusing on the *benefits* of the product. Repeatedly, I'm complimenting their decision to have made the purchase, as I go through the resale:

> "Margie, I don't know if you remember, but this product includes a travel benefit that pays up to $2,500 per trip anywhere in the country if you were to go through cancer and also allows you to bring a direct family member. Isn't that amazing? By the way, you *already* have this in the plan that you purchased. What a great decision to get that for your family!"

Make your clients feel great about the purchase that they made from you. Whether I reservice a client 30 days or three years later (as I said, I'll try to see my clients multiple times a year in some cases), I always want them to feel like Einstein for having purchased our plans.

Acknowledge the Elephant in the Room
You want to sell the client something else. You know it, they know it, and it's best to simply acknowledge it.

As I'm reservicing and reselling my client on the product they've already purchased, I'll casually reference one of the plans that they *didn't* get from me:

> "So, Margie, the way this works for our cancer plan is the same way that it works for our accident plan. I remember when I saw you, you said you wanted to hold off on that plan for a bit, so now that I'm back, I'll give you another look before I wrap up. ***I wouldn't be a good sales guy if I didn't have something new to show you, right?!*** Before I get into that, though, let me focus on the rest of your cancer plan, because that's the main reason I'm here."

In this example, while I'm doing a reservice demonstration of the cancer plan, I'm casually hinting that I'm planning to give her another demo on another plan, with the intention of selling her. I do it in a lighthearted way, and even make that comment about "being a good salesman." The bottom line is that it clears the air about something that she assumed I was going to broach anyway. The other key is that by including it *during* my reservice of the cancer plan, it gave me permission to go into it afterward, without an awkward transition.

Offer New Options
When making the transition from reservicing their current plan or product to trying to sell them a new plan or product, remember to include a new buying atmosphere. Keep it casual, but just as we covered in the earlier chapters, if you do *not* include this, you must keep coming back again and again to get a final decision. Don't be deceived that just because your client bought from you before that they'll remember that they need to decide after you show them something new.

> "Margie, as I mentioned, let's take a quick look at the accident plan that you wanted to reconsider. If you like it, great, it's simple to get it added onto your other plan(s). It's like getting Girl Scout cookies: easy. If you still don't think it's a fit, that's not a problem either. Just let me know one way or another if you'd like to add that on. Fair enough?"

Keep it simple! The more complicated you make things, they more complicated your client will think that the decision-making process will be. Give an effective, quick presentation of whatever else you think is important to offer, and close.

Get New Referrals
I can't emphasize this enough: **GET MORE REFERRALS!** No matter how effective you were on your last visit getting referrals from this client, don't hesitate to repeat the entire process. It may be the same individual, but it's a different scenario. It's not the first time you've met. You have established a relationship, and this opens new doors. You'll find that existing clients will:

- Mention your products and how good they are while they're at work, school, PTA, church, to other parents, relatives, and so on.
- Call their referrals ahead of time to announce that you're coming.
- Purchase your product or service for others as gifts.
- Have you come and sell within their businesses.

Building a strong network will reveal new avenues that weren't available in your first meeting, and referrals are the catalyst to your growth.

Chapter 16

"You are not here merely to make a living. You are here in order to enable the world to live more amply, with greater vision, with a finer spirit of hope and achievement. You are here to enrich the world, and you impoverish yourself if you forget the errand."

Woodrow Wilson

Various Methods of Direct Sales

Direct sales immediately makes one think of to door-to-sales: referral-to-referral selling, setting up appointments on the phone, consumer web conferences / virtual and attending networking groups, to name a few. There are many forms of selling, and this book concentrates on the key principles on which to build relationships and close deals. Rather than reviewing myriad sales approaches, I'll touch on just a few ideas to enhance your current knowledge and, more importantly, keep you *efficient* in filling your sales funnel.

T-Approach

The T-approach goes by many names but was so named because it describes a door-to-door approach when your main contact isn't available. Imagine you're trying to reservice a client or visit a referral who is the third house on the left of a certain block, but no one's home. From an aerial view, if you look at the houses directly to the left and right of that prospect, as well as the one right across the street, you create the shape of a T. If you include the houses next to the one across the street, you might change the name to the four-leaf-clover approach.

The T-approach is, hands down, one of my favorite approaches. First, it may seem like cold calling, but it's not, and you'll see why. Second, it generates efficiency when you realize that your prospect isn't home. Third, it calls on people to help you, and you'll find that most people really want to help when they're given the opportunity.

The T-approach is quite simple. You are calling on the closest house to your prospect that seems to have a sign of life, perhaps cars in the drive or, even better, someone outside. The goal is to find out when it's best to call back on your prospect and, in the meantime, try to get a new sale with this neighbor. The process goes something like this: Jog over to the person you see and wave as you approach.

> "Hi! I didn't mean to catch you off-guard. I'm not even here to see *you*; I'm trying to catch up with Bruce and Julia next door. Bruce's brother Mark suggested I come by and see them, but they've been impossible to catch. Do you know if it's best to reach them in the mornings or are evenings better?"

They reply, "Oh, they're never here during the day. They usually aren't back until five or maybe even later."

Meanwhile, I'm jotting this information in my notes and thanking them for their help, all the while, starting to establish rapport with them.

> "I noticed your University of Texas flag as I ran up. Were you a Longhorn?"

Find something to connect with, using the same basic skills that you learned during the chapter on rapport. When you feel you've made a solid connection, transition into the second approach that you learned.

> "So, have you heard about me yet? Oh, I'm sorry. My name is Dan Janjigian, and I work for Company X. I've been working here in town for

a while, and Mark made me promise to catch Bruce and Julia while I'm here. I'm just seeing friends and family, so I guess you folks would kind of qualify! I've only got a few minutes; do you have a place to sit down?"

Break eye contact, wipe your feet, and go on in.

This approach works better than I can ever explain. I call it my *ninja* approach because it hits the prospect unexpectedly. Most people whom you approach are summing you up when you first meet them. In this approach, you're letting them off the hook immediately by letting them know that you're *not* there to see *them*. Not only that, but you also solidify that fact by telling them who you *are* there to see, and the people that referred you to see them. This creates major clout in the conversation because you're *supposed* to be there, you know their neighbors, and if they know their neighbors at all, they probably also knows Bruce's brother who sent you over. When you go through this approach asking for help, you can bet that most times, that's exactly what you're going to get!

Transitioning to the second approach is also easy after you've built a little rapport. You'll sit down immediately with many of these prospects (they want to know what everyone around them seems to be getting). Also, if they're busy or don't have much time, you can still usually schedule a solid appointment.

This becomes a powerful help in your sales process with Bruce and Julia. Whether or not the neighbor buys, when you meet with Bruce and Julia, you have added a name to use other than Bruce's brother. Imagine how strong this is when that neighbor is also a customer? You are building out an area in a very tight way.

I mentioned earlier how this is also very efficient. You are not driving around all day yet never talking to a prospect. Even veteran salespeople struggle with this. By learning effective T-approach techniques, you become efficient, performing sales-driven activities nearly every time you get out of your car. Never drive around without talking to prospects. You may feel busy, but you're not creating any business behind the wheel.

Business to Business

Business-to-business (B2B) selling is its own beast. In addition to the techniques already presented, two B2B aspects are unique: identifying the gatekeeper and working within a crowd.

There is one major caveat. If you're selling big ticket items, you can use many of the earlier concepts. B2B selling, however, is more in line with products and services that you would sell to mom and pop style companies. Enterprise deals would be much larger, and a guide I highly recommend to anyone is *Pitch Anything* by Oren Klaff. If you're selling larger ticket items, especially those that may require multiple calls on the business, this is a great reference.

For our purposes, B2B sales might be smaller products: insurance, payroll, credit card processing, stationery, advertising, shipping solutions, bookkeeping, and so on. Thousands of products and services are sold daily, and small businesses comprise most buyers, so definitely attack this market with gusto.

Again, we're going to discuss concepts rather than specific solutions, because when you're calling on nearly any business, you'll face the same issues.

Gatekeeper

The beauty of working small to midsized businesses is that the *gatekeeper* is often the person that you want to call on anyway. For example, instead of a classic admin at the front desk whose job is to filter through your pitch and see if you are worth her boss's time, you may be speaking to the boss herself! Your job is to have an effective approach to get a conversation started.

First, anticipate what the person at the front desk is expecting. Most people who walk into businesses are there to do what? To do business! They're looking to spend money on whatever the business sells. If it's a restaurant, it's food. If it's a tire shop, they're selling tires. When you walk in, take an interest *first* in their business to create an immediate rapport.

Chapter 16

"What a great place! If you don't mind me asking, how long have you folks been operating here?"

When approaching small businesses, don't just jump into the reason that you're there. That's how every amateur does it, and that's not you. People are people, and it's relationships that lead to effective networking.

Second, briefly review what you're doing, and figure out who you need to talk to. Whether a business is slow or busy, people have things to do. Unless you are proposing a money-making activity, you're way down their list of things they want to spend time on. A sharp elevator pitch and a transition to how you're going to follow up can get what you need and leave a positive impression to help you get welcomed back.

"I don't mean to catch you when you're so busy, but I was just with one of my clients next door, and I didn't realize you folks were located here. I work with Jerry Townes and his staff on their benefit programs, and we specialize in companies that are your size. I know right now is probably not the best time to get into details, but who would I reach out to for a quick introduction?"

"You'd probably want to talk to Barbara Flores. We're not really that big, but she's the owner."

"Great," I reply, "Could I get Barbara's card from you? What is your name?"

"Cindy."

"Thanks, Cindy. Please let her know that Dan will drop her a quick line with some information."

That's it. Less is more in businesses, and you'll avoid getting pushed aside for paying clients that are waiting. Follow up with an email, followed by a call, to try to set a time to meet with Barbara at her convenience. Usually, first thing in the morning between 7 to 8 a.m. is best for most business owners.

Springboarding—C2C to B2B and Back (*Consumer to Consumer / Business to Business*)

Springboarding is a term I coined for bouncing between residential and business markets. Almost always, referrals from clients are to fellow employees at their place of business. Some clients own small to midsized businesses, and I'll discuss the benefits of offering these services to their employees.

Working businesses is key, but in some markets such as insurance, it's extremely important to transition your business clients back into a residential setting. Here's why:

In insurance, most employees know that once they leave the business, they also leave their benefits. Their employer had been paying for them, or their plan was tied to their payroll. Generally, employees are part of a group plan, meaning they're effectively leasing their benefits for the duration of their employment. The loyalty of the plan is tied directly to the employer.

Today, we work in a world where most employees no longer stay with one company for 40 years. People tend to bounce between jobs and employers and even different careers. Therefore, it's important for direct salespeople to create a relationship with these employees, separate from their employers. We even track this profitability within our business, and simply put, a residential sale is nearly three times more profitable than a business sale. If you're in a business that deals with long-term residual income, where would you want to see your time spent?

The solution is to simply use the reservicing techniques described in the previous chapter. When an employee signs up with us through work, we take extra pains to reservice them at home. This doesn't always work, as you may have employees that live out of town and sometimes even out of state or country, but in most cases, you can see these clients in the comfort of their home, surrounded by their spouse and kids, and establish a relationship that is separate from the employer.

In a recent situation, a major company that I was doing business with had shut down one of its offices because of a steep drop in gas prices. During the transition, I retained most of my clientele because they felt comfortable calling me to ask what their options were and what they could do. Their relationship was directly with me, and that made all the difference.

Chapter 17

"Nothing can stop the man with the right mental attitude from achieving his goal. Nothing on earth can help the man with the wrong attitude"

Thomas Jefferson

Setting Up Business Enrollments

Enrollments are a lot of fun to set up with companies, but if you're new to direct sales, especially if you're in a commission-only scenario, don't rely on this as your only source of income. Enrollments can be very lucrative but also very challenging if you haven't learned how best to navigate them. Also, they seldom happen on *your* schedule.

This is another area where the concepts of the sale are more important than any specific verbiage to use in the process. Depending on what you're selling, employers might suggest that you set up a booth, make a presentation at a meeting, or set up in a conference room. Employers have asked me to come in at the same time my competitors were walking in. I've had them ask me for RFPs (Requests for Proposals). Some wanted me to just stop by their company picnics or even talk to their employees who were away on contracting jobs.

Your job is to run your business like a business and work with the employer to find the best situation for you, them, and the employees. It's no good to anyone if you set up a booth at an event if it's not conducive to your sales system. If you have no chance to explain your product and its benefits, then trying to present is a waste of time and resources. As much as you know how best to present your product, the employer knows how best to get in front of employees when they're most willing to hear what you have to say. Work together; don't blindly accept what the employer offers as the solution for your presentation.

Time and Space

When you're working an enrollment, time and space are the two biggest factors to success. Time with your prospects. How much of it do you have? Is the employer okay with you speaking to them on the clock? How much time do you reasonably have to speak with each prospect? How many hours and days do you have to get through all their employees? How many locations will you be working and when?

Space is a function of where you'll be presenting or working. Will you be doing both? Where can you meet one on one or in groups? Do you need paperwork filled out? Physical paperwork, or online? Is any technology required during the presentation? Is a computer necessary to sign someone up? Do you need a private office for privileged discussions, or is an open conference room enough? Is it just you, or will you have associates working with you?

Business vs. Residential Pitch

In most business settings, you'll have to abridge what you might cover residentially. In a residential setting, you can relax and establish a lot of trust through rapport. Much of this is already established by the fact that the employer has invited you in. This credibility goes a long way, although you still need to find ways to connect quickly. A powerful means to this is by establishing connections through co-workers that you may have already met with or sold to.

Make a quick demonstration. Except for some products and services, find an effective way to get your prospects in and out in ten to twenty minutes. Perhaps you work with union employees, chambers of commerce, schools, safety meetings, county municipalities, and so on. It's hard to see everyone in groups with large numbers of members if you're not extremely efficient. Use survey forms that track the prospects' interest in certain products and let everyone know that they're required to fill one out, *even if* they're not interested (this ensures that you haven't accidentally missed anyone).

Believe in what you're doing, and your confidence will close the most deals for you. Employees will see you as an extension of their company, even if you're new to everyone in management. Be confident because you've been given the keys to the castle and you deserve to be there.

Finally, know your paperwork inside and out. With enrollments, you must bridge your company's paperwork with that of the company that you're working with. Figure out in advance what you're going to need and how to overcome any objections that may arise in getting it. For example:

Because our premiums are withdrawn monthly from my clients' personal accounts and because I try to keep my relationships directly with my clients and not through their place of business, I rarely do traditional enrollments. In traditional enrollments, payments come directly out of the client's payroll.

When I meet with a prospect who becomes a client, I know that I'll need their banking information. Because most people don't carry a checkbook and I don't want to try to track them down later, I'll meet with the head of HR to see what paperwork is needed to get that information directly from the company. Sometimes this is simply a one-page authorization that the client signs as I'm finalizing their paperwork, or sometimes the signed application is enough. My job is to figure that out ahead of time so that I'm not unprofessional in the process as I'm getting new clients signed up.

You've heard this again and again: Make sure to run your business like a business!

Chapter 18

"We judge ourselves by our intensions and others by their actions"

Stephen Covey

The Grass Always Looks Greener

Why do direct salespeople jump from company to company? As of this writing, I've been working in direct sales for nearly 30 years. During that time, I've observed that salespeople tend to fit into two categories: those who are consistent in their efforts and own homes out on the lake, and the ones who constantly jump to the next best thing (in their mind), a seemingly endless cycle. That's the "grass is always greener" philosophy.

I don't think this is any truer than in insurance. We recruit new agents to envision for themselves a life that lets them retire with a substantial residual income while enjoying the flexibility to live well, travel, and so on. This career also provides help for people when they really need it. The irony is that most people who work in our industry quit in just a couple of months. Why is that?

I think it's because of two reasons: the type of sale and a lack of discipline.

Inside vs. Outside Selling

The chasm between these two types of sales is vast. They may sound similar but they're not. Most salespeople have done inside selling such as:

- Call center
- Software sales (inbound calls)
- Car lot
- Waiter or waitress

In each example, success can come easier than in outside sales. For example, I call to get the newest copy of Adobe Photoshop, and if you're a well-trained salesperson, you upsell me to a bigger package with all sorts of additional bells and whistles. Or maybe you work on a car lot and you upsell me into an $80K GMC truck.

In either case, I came to *you*. I called for the software, or I walked on the lot looking for a new truck. Someone else marketed the service or product that you're selling, advertised your call center phone number, or enticed me to walk on the car lot.

Direct sales, by nature, is *outside* sales, which constitutes true salesmanship. We sell to people who were not looking for our products and, in some cases, didn't know they existed. They weren't thinking about making a purchase until we sat down with them.

Direct salespeople, consequently, are some of the most pursued in the industry. We generate business where none existed. We create something from nothing. It is said that a salesperson creates 21 new jobs, and that is something to applaud. In my business, nobody would have a job if our salespeople weren't putting new products on the books every day. What would Customer Service be servicing? From what accounts would Accounts Receivable be collecting? Who would Marketing be marketing to?

We run a marathon, not a sprint. Every sales job gets easier over time; that's simple logic. What's not logical to some is that any sales job is *tough* in the beginning, even if your sales pedigree is amazing. You must become familiar with new sales talks, new product benefits, new hierarchies and corporate structures, perhaps even new rules and regulations. The truth is, we should be thankful that it's tough in the beginning; if it weren't, we wouldn't get paid as well as we do.

Salespeople will always be highly recruited. It's an honor to know that we, as managers and leaders, are creating top tier sales folks, while at the same time, it's a shame to know that, in most cases, they'll find themselves starting over and over at company after company until they finally realize that they can't grow into a mighty oak if they keep pulling up their roots. Creating a plan and abiding by it allows you to grow beyond what you think is possible.

Lack of Discipline
This is the second and most obvious reason I see people fail in direct sales.

We all dream of a world where we won't be micromanaged. We want the trust and autonomy that comes from doing our job on our own. As much as we want this, most of the world *needs* someone at work who holds them accountable or "writes them up" if they show up late or try to leave early. If we didn't, why wouldn't we sleep in another hour or go home earlier than we should?

Discipline accounts for all of that. With a military or athletic background, you might already have a leg up because it's been drilled into you through basic training that you have to disassemble a rifle a thousand times before they'll let you shoot it. As an athlete, you must go to training camp and do strength training, memorize the play book, run patterns, and so on, before you ever play a game. Thousands of hours go into practicing a dive that takes under three seconds for an athlete to take home their Olympic gold.

Discipline is a commitment to doing the things necessary to be successful even when you don't feel like it. It's working, even though all your appointments canceled. It's finding a way, even though you awoke to a flat tire. It's getting out there, even though there's a death in the family.

We run businesses. Ask yourself, if you worked for a major corporation like Microsoft or Apple, how many days off, if any, would you take for that flat tire, or even a family emergency? There are exceptions to every rule, but I can't tell you the number of people that I've seen take weeks off because of some of the situations on that list. Would you still have your Microsoft job? Would your previous full-time job take you back? You need to run your business like a business, and that requires discipline in every aspect of what you do. Life happens, *but* it also goes on.

Purpose and Vision

Whether you're a business veteran or a novice, your purpose is the factor that takes you where you want to go. By the way—NO—money should not be your primary purpose. Now, your purpose can be something that requires money, but be specific.

Your purpose must be something that you can target. It can be, and often is, tied to money. For example, it could be to pay down a specific debt. It can be for putting away enough for your kids' college education. Maybe it's to set a company record or achieve your personal best. Maybe it's to enjoy the flexibility to take your spouse on a four-day vacation without worrying about work.

You can put your purpose on a vision board or even tape it to your dashboard as an incentive when you're out in the field. It should be something tangible so you can look at it or remind yourself of it regularly. Remind yourself of your purpose every morning when you get up and several times throughout the day. Stick it in the frame of your bathroom mirror. Write it and frame it by your desk. Your purpose is what keeps you working when you don't feel like it. *Everyone* goes through those feelings. When your purpose is strong, it will outweigh your fear or your desire to do something that's not in line with your ultimate goals.

Chapter 19

"If you have integrity, nothing else matters.
If you don't have integrity,
nothing else matters"

Alan K. Simpson

Integrity

We've covered a lot of technical information throughout this book, but for most readers, technical is a small fraction of what you need to be successful in direct sales. As highlighted in the first few chapters, your discipline and keeping to the task at hand is the key to your success in any sales career. It's what separates the successful from the unsuccessful in nearly every aspect of life. Getting out there and staying out there are tied to the goals that you set, as well as the purpose that you have for pursuing a sales career in the first place. These items are ruled by one thing: integrity.

Your *word* is the definition of integrity. Your word defines you as an individual. Integrity is committing to the things that you've said that you'll do in an uncompromising fashion. Integrity is valuing your commitment to something as the bond that holds the key to who you are and what the world can expect from you.

Integrity is not just committing to the things that you say, but also committing to the things that you expect of yourself. If you marry or are in a serious relationship, you may not make a vow to be faithful, but if you believe that's part of being in a committed relationship, then cheating on your partner shows a lack of integrity.

Promising your child that you'll be there for their soccer game, and not being there because you had to work is a lack of integrity.

If you're the person who has an excuse as to why you're always late, you have an integrity issue.

If you missed work because you were sick, but you really weren't "that sick," you lack integrity.

If you commit to a sales position, and you find that you're not sticking to the schedule that you committed to, you lack integrity.

Lacking integrity doesn't make you a bad person, it just means that what you commit to isn't as reliable as someone who has integrity.

In my opinion, integrity is the *number one reason* that people fail in direct sales. It has nothing to do with their desire to succeed or their belief that they are capable, but it has everything to do with their willingness to stick to their commitments.

Most solid sales organizations have a trainer or manager to help solidify your schedule and determine what to do at every moment within that schedule. In some cases, your schedule might be a 9 to 5 standard workday, but for most direct sales contractors, their schedule is much more flexible and must be written out weekly. In either case, integrity is found in committing to the "controllables," which are the hours that you will work, and the success factors, which are the things that you commit to doing within those hours.

Sounds easy, but it's not. You should be happy that it's not; otherwise everyone would do it, and it wouldn't pay as well! The reality is that this is where most people are filtered out of direct sales and all the wonderful opportunities that attracted them to the industry to begin with. Don't fool yourself, all those amazing things they promised you could achieve actually do exist, but the majority of people won't achieve those goals because they're unwilling to do the things they committed to do in order to truly succeed.

This is one of the final chapters of this book to encourage you to understand the following:

You can spend all the time and money in the world to build your business. You can memorize all the closing techniques and sales skills that exist. You can be the best talker in town or the most naturally talented salesperson that anyone has ever seen. None of it makes the least bit of difference if you don't do the things that you say you're going to do. In direct sales, this can be the integrity that you exhibit to your customers in the promises that you make to them. More directly, it's oftentimes related to the immense failure rates for salespeople in nearly every direct sales team.

Now, things happen. They happen to all of us, and they're legitimate. Family members pass, kids get sick, car accidents happen. The question, as we posed earlier, is, if you worked for a major corporation, and your job or salary was on the line, would you still find yourself unavailable to perform on time as you'd committed? If the answer is yes, then consider two things:

1. Maintain your integrity. When you realize you're unable to fulfill your commitment, immediately inform all affected parties so that they can adjust accordingly, and that the least damage is inflicted by your absence. Most people believe that it's better to ask for forgiveness later, but that's just not true. Maintaining your integrity is retaining other people's belief in your ability to perform. Sometimes, even one lapse can have irreparable consequences.

2. Regain your integrity. Unavoidable things happen, and you cannot always keep your promises. Maybe a chemical truck flipped in front of your car on the highway, and you were stuck in a two-hour traffic jam, and it happened to be on the morning that your husband accidentally took your phone with him. What do you do in situations that are truly unavoidable? Again, as soon as possible, coordinate with all affected members of your group, and:

a. Acknowledge your break in Integrity. Take responsibility for the fact that you didn't deliver as promised, and proactively address this with the members of your team. Don't wait for them to come to you, even if you consider it a minor deal. It's a powerful message when anyone takes responsibility for their actions.
b. Share your understanding of how your break must have affected the group. Nobody cares about your reasons or your apologies, but they do care that you understand the consequences of the situation, *even* if it's justifiable.
c. Commit to specifics that you'll put into place to make sure that the cause of your break doesn't occur again. In this case, which is an extreme, it may be to simply make sure that you take your phone and put it in your handbag as your first act when you get out of bed in the morning. If you're constantly 15 minutes late for work, you might commit to changing your alarm clock to go off 30 minutes earlier every morning.

Teddy Roosevelt summed up integrity better than I ever could:

"It is not the critic who counts; not the man who points out how the strong man stumbles, or where the doer of deeds could have done them better. The credit belongs to the man who is actually in the arena, whose face is marred by dust and sweat and blood; who strives valiantly; who errs; who comes short again and again, because there is no effort without error and shortcoming; but who does actually strive to do the deeds; who knows great enthusiasms, the great devotions; who spends himself in a worthy cause; who at the best knows in the end the triumph of high achievement, and who at the worst, if he fails, at least fails while daring greatly, so that his place shall never be with those cold and timid souls who neither know victory nor defeat."

Integrity is doing what you said that you would do and giving your best effort while doing it.

Chapter 20

"There is no greater agony than bearing an untold story inside you"

Maya Angelou

Let's Go!

This is a book three decades in the making. There's no way to account for every situation that you'll encounter in the field, but to establish a strong foundation, you must start using and implementing the concepts covered in these chapters. After you've finished reading, review the specific chapters that you feel could be most helpful.

Examine the objections you're encountering. Are they consistently the same? For example, if your clients are uncomfortable giving you their account information or writing you a check, that could be a trust issue. Improve your use of names and establishing rapport. Do you keep encountering the spouse/procrastination objection? Maybe you need to work on establishing a stronger buying atmosphere. These chapters were built as sections in and of themselves to use for your own sales, or even to assist you in working with the growth of your sales teams.

Direct sales is the oldest profession out there (think about it!) and is arguably the most important because of how it stimulates the economy and other jobs. You'll seldom hear about a company laying off its top salespeople.

They're the lifeblood of what runs all businesses. It's a fraternity of go-getters and captains of industry. It's heralded by many of the world's top earners, and many of them have shared their stories about the necessity of direct selling to get them to where they are today. It's unique because it doesn't require a degree; everyone can do it, but not many will. Direct sales pays at high levels because the men and women who do it are literally paid what they're worth; not what someone believes they should be paid. It inspires entrepreneurs and rewards visionaries.

Be confident and believe in what you sell and how you sell it. As a final thought, remember the underlying message of Dr. Albert Gray's book, *The Common Denominator of Success:*

> "The secret of **success** of every man who has ever been **successful** lies in the fact that he formed the habit of doing things that failures don't like to do."

Make a life for yourself that's extraordinary… the world of direct sales!

Chapter 21

"No matter how successful you are or how clever or crafty, your business and its future are in the hand of the people you hire"

Akio Morita, Sony Corp. co-founder

Bonus for Managers

Most direct sales organizations grow from the inside out. Salespeople are encouraged and often rewarded for recruiting new talent and transitioning into management roles in parallel with their sales responsibilities. Whether you've recruited your own team or are in a position of leadership over sales professionals, here are a few key ideas to help you with your direct sales team.

Setting the Bar

Your people will commonly do about 80% of what they see you do in the field, so get out there and show off! The best sales trainers will have a recruit watch and learn from them for at least a few days in the field. If your systems of success require new agents to make 30 contacts every day, then go out and show them how to make 40. If you'd like your agents to give five presentations a day, show them how to make eight. Let them see you sell more than the daily average and let them see you work later than they thought they were supposed to.

I once took an agent out to the field who was determined that the best way to sell our product was a classic 9 to 5 schedule. He wanted to build a "sales empire" but, in my opinion, was working like someone's employee, not someone that was sacrificing for success. After starting at 10 a.m. after our team meetings, we left our last house at 2 a.m. the next morning. We had our last three appointments (two of them purchased) starting at 11:30 p.m., and we finished our day together after 16 hours in the field. What do you think the message was when he was usually cutting off at 5 p.m.?

You create a business culture for your new agents. When a new agent transitions into direct sales, they generally don't have anything to compare it to, and what they see from you is what they're going to assume is expected of them, so set a high bar. When the day gets tough, keep your chin up and don't complain about the one that "got away." If you have a day where nobody buys, let them know that it's just the Law of Averages, and it always balances out.

When you're training, it's tempting to show off how good you are, but stick closely to the basics. For example, if you're a veteran in the business, you've probably become very flexible in the way you present, but when you're training, go to great pains to train as close as you can to the way your recruit was taught. New agents need to believe that the system works—if they get in front of enough prospects.

Memorize / Internalize / Personalize

All effective systems include sales presentations and scripts that cover closes, answering objections, price buildups, and buying atmospheres. These should all be written out so that someone can learn them word for word. Your best opportunity to succeed requires memorizing your presentation materials, and the same holds true for your recruits. Therefore, do not freestyle when you're training a new salesperson. They need to see that simply using the words they were given will work if they use them with conviction and take the time to memorize.

Next, internalize the demonstration. Take what you have memorized and become so comfortable with the material that if a prospect asks questions or gets you off track, you can easily transition back to where you left off. Your trainees should reach this point quickly so they can begin to pay better attention to their prospects.

Personalizing is when your agents begin to turn into sales professionals. Now they can readily bring their personality, stories, and names into the sales process. A good foundation gets someone here quickly, and it's generally when your teams profess that they no longer feel like robots.

Sales Meetings

Meeting should be based in two distinct areas: technical and emotional.

Technical Training gets into the specifics of how to get better at the actual business. Take any concept in this book and concentrate on breaking it down. Teach your group how to become a master of referrals. Show how to become better at approaching businesses. Also include items outside of what we've discussed. For example, how can you use the Internet to help track down referrals? What is ReferenceUSA and how might it help to target better clients?

Emotional Training speaks more to *why* we're doing what we're doing and *how* to deal with the feelings that we deal with in the field. Hold meetings about "purpose" and run exercises on why they decided to transition into performance-based sales. Discuss what it means to be average vs. amazing; perhaps a talk on the difference between success and significance. Emotional training is one that I love to see woven into every meeting, even if it's just a small idea to think about. You can have an entire meeting on emotional training and skip technical, but you probably shouldn't have a strictly technical meeting without covering some emotional ground.

Follow Up with New Agents

Keep your thumb on the pulse of your sales team. Big sales numbers don't guarantee that someone's going to stick around, and low numbers don't necessarily mean that someone isn't working. One of my top sales recruits had almost no sales in his first full month of working with me, but he was coachable and had laid a strong foundation making demonstration after demonstration. His first full year in the business he broke the company record and then broke his own record the following year.

Conversely, agents with amazing first months left for other job opportunities because they felt they hadn't been looked after enough. The rule of thumb is this: Prioritize your time on those you know are working. You can't be everywhere at once, so decide, based on effort, who needs you the most. Make sure that everyone on your team gets your personal attention, especially face time, to create a tribe mentality in which they'll want to excel.

Watch their success factors. Focus on the activities that you know are laying the groundwork for long-term success. If you focus on results, your people will rollercoaster not just in their sales, but in their feelings of how they think they're performing. If your focus is instead on success factors such as calls, approaches, demonstrations, or hours, then you can celebrate consistent wins with your sales teams.

The 50/50 Rule of Sales/Management

There are many books on management, and this bonus section touches on key points for anyone who's working with a direct sales team. The reason I included this chapter is to drive home one key point:

If your company allows, work immediately to split your income between your personal sales and the income you create from building your team based on how you get compensated. For example, if you're making 80% of your income from personal sales, then spend no more than 20% of your time outside of that role. Many organizations will market your ability to begin building from Day 1, and in most organizations, your long-term growth will come from the success of your organization, not the success of your personal sales. You should never be able to outsell personally what your organization can sell collectively, so make this a priority from your first day, but don't forget what drives most of your income. As you start to see that percentage change, you can continue to change where you place your effort.

Other key reasons to start building your organization quickly:

Chapter 21

1) Your personal sales will go up. Why? Because you'll work harder to show your team the "right way." Think of a marathon. You always run faster if you're running with someone because if they speed up, you'll try to keep up.
11) Sales teams don't quit, just salespeople. You're stronger with your tribe!
12) It's more fun! Direct sales is *hard,* but it gets easier with time. Play hard and do it with the people that you brought along for the ride. Remember the rule of the Inverse Pyramid (from my good friend John Wayne Southerland): "Your efforts in direct sales and team building are like a pyramid that's upside down. When you begin, your success is like the bottom of the pyramid that's touching the ground. There's not much of it. But as time goes by, you work your way up the pyramid, and your success gets greater and greater, while your effort decreases as the job becomes easier."

Time and Effort 100% controls how long it takes you to move up that pyramid!

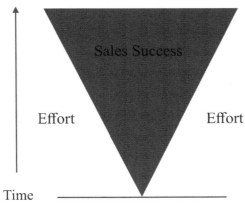

Conclusion

The world is constantly changing, and those challenges will open new avenues for sales, but the fundamental structure discussed in these pages will never change. From technology to pandemics, we may need to meet via the Internet or phone, as opposed to in person, but it's still direct sales and the same rules apply.

After working and training in sales for the past three decades, I can honestly say that it's one of the best, most rewarding skills that you can hone. Sales is a superpower that every one of us has the capability to tap into, and with it you can significantly change your world and the world for others.

Feedback on The Book on Selling:
"This amazing book brings all the concepts of selling together in one place. Whether you're new to sales or a veteran in the field, these ideas will help you unlock your special abilities to succeed. Read it, apply it, and let it change your life. No sales library should be without it."

Brian Tracy,
Author/Speaker/Consultant

"Janjigian suggests the same level of preparation is necessary for a sales call that made him an Olympic athlete competing at the world's highest level. *The Book on Selling* takes you through the reasons for all the preparation involved in selling including how to sell during a pandemic."

David Abramson
Named Top 50 in High Tech PR by PRWeek Magazine

As Chairman of OneAccord & several additional businesses through Solomons Fund, we deal with multiple sales teams – business to business, business to consumer, direct, channel, inside & outside, etc.

Chapter 21

I can't think of a better GUIDE TO SALES than <u>The Book on Selling</u> by Dan Janjigian. I've read several books and have additionally been through courses on the profession of sales, YET most don't deal with the foundation – WHY. Why sales? Why is it important? Why are some more successful than others, yet sharing similar talents and similar skills? Most deal with technique – which can often be honestly described as manipulation or strategy for a win – but they miss the understanding of motivation, differentiation, & conviction. Dan takes it to another step, then moving into the fundamentals. These fundamentals transcend industries, markets, geographies, products and services.

This should be the first book in one's sales library.

Jeff Rogers
Chariman, OneAccord

"Of all the books, seminars training courses and podcasts, *The Book on Selling* has become the indispensable direct sales Bible. Every person in direct sales can implement these strategies and succeed NOW."

Rick Altig,
Agency Owner, Altig International

Made in the USA
Middletown, DE
03 December 2022

16427955R00082